HOW TO WRITE YOUR FIRST NOVEL

THE STRESS-FREE GUIDE TO WRITING FICTION FOR BEGINNERS

M.L. RONN

CONTENTS

WHAT YOU'LL LEARN FROM THIS BOOK

NOVEMBER 15, 2011 is one day in my writing career I'll never forget.

I was sitting in my bedroom, nursing a mug of hot chocolate, as I stared at my laptop, at a blinking cursor.

It was snowing outside.

My wife was watching *Hell's Kitchen* in the living room, and Gordon Ramsay was yelling so loudly he might as well have been yelling at me.

"Come on!"

"Get a grip!"

"Are you checked out?"

I had been staring at my work-in-progress for over an hour, and I couldn't do it anymore.

I shut my laptop lid and sighed.

This was the day I failed at writing my first novel.

I was participating in National Novel Writing Month (NaNoWriMo) with the goal of writing 50,000 words by November 30, and I didn't even make it halfway through the month. At only 15,000 words, I was too far behind to recover. I had written in coffee shops, at the library, during breaks at work —and the words just wouldn't come.

I told myself that I couldn't be a writer, and I truly believed it.

I gave up on writing that day.

In the months that followed, I was miserable. I couldn't tell what was worse—writing and failing at it, or not writing at all!

In July 2012—eight months later—after a lovely dinner date with my wife, I fell ill with what I thought was food poisoning.

I went to the hospital and didn't leave for a month. I'll spare you the details, but I contracted a deadly illness and could have died.

On that hospital bed, I really thought about my life.

I thought about the manuscript I had given up on.

I thought about being a writer again.

And on that bed, in the middle of morphine hallucinations, with an IV in my arm and a plate of jiggly hospital Jell-O on my lap, I swore that I would be a writer again. For real this time.

I made a full recovery, thank goodness. I eventually finished my first novel, publishing it on January 5, 2014.

And here I am now, writing this book for you.

WHO I AM AND WHY I WROTE THIS BOOK

At the time of this writing, I've written over 40 books—30 of them being novels.

I run a YouTube channel called *Author Level Up* where I publish weekly videos with advice for writers.

I also co-host two popular podcasts for writers.

And most importantly, I've managed to do all of this while

working a full-time job, raising a family, and attending law school classes in the evenings.

I've come a long way since that fateful day in 2011, where nothing seemed possible. When I look back at my early days, I'm amazed at how woefully unprepared I was to write a novel at the start of my career.

I wish someone would have told me how hard it is to write your first few novels.

I wish someone would have told me step-by-step how to write a novel, what apps to buy, what to write, what to do if I got stuck.

There are plenty of writing resources out there, but few of them address the "technical" part of being a writer.

For example, when it comes to writer's block, you're likely to hear:

- "Just put your butt in the chair and do it!"
- "You can do it. I believe in you."
- "Just imagine your finished novel…"

I don't know about you, but I've never found that kind of advice helpful or productive.

What I needed would have been something like this:

- "When you get stuck, consider this. If that doesn't work, do this."
- "Here's exactly what to write in your opening chapter. After that, write this."

That kind of structured guidance is exactly what most writers need early in their careers.

In writing this book, I wanted to write the book I wish I had when I wrote my first novel. I don't believe in fluffy writing; I believe in being honest and direct, because you didn't pick up this book to read fluff.

I want you to finish your book!

But more importantly, I want you to learn how to write a novel quickly and well, because it's a skill that will serve you well for the rest of your writing career.

WHO THIS BOOK IS FOR

This book is for fiction writers who write in the major fiction genres: science fiction, fantasy, romance, mysteries, thrillers, and westerns. If you write in those genres (or in any subgenres within them), then this book is a perfect fit for you.

This book is primarily for those writing their first novel. If you've written a novel or two and still want some help, this book will help you too.

Throughout this book, I will assume that you have a basic understanding of the different elements of fiction such as plot, character, setting, etc. I will also assume that you have a grasp on basic spelling, grammar, and punctuation.

OVERVIEW OF THIS BOOK

You can read this book straight through or jump to the sections that interest you.

- **The Frequently Asked Questions** section
  contains the most common questions I get from

writers about writing a novel. Even if you think you know the common questions and answers, don't skip it, because I have a different perspective than most.

- The **Tools** section contains my recommendations for the apps and tools I believe are necessary to write a novel in today's publishing market.
- The **Planning Your Novel** section will give you step-by-step instructions on exactly what to do before you start writing.
- The **Writing Your Novel** section will give you step-by-step instructions on what to write at every major plot point. There are checklists, do's, don'ts, and case studies from my own experience. This section is the most technical in the book, but my hope is that it will be eye-opening and by itself worth the price of the book.
- The **Revising Your Novel** section will give you step-by-step instructions on how to edit your book so you can get it ready for publication.
- The **Resources** section contains links to all of the resources I mention in this book, all in one place for your convenience.

This is a short book for a reason, but it *will* be thorough. My goal is to keep things simple for you so that you can get started right away.

It's easy to get overwhelmed as a new novelist, but writing doesn't have to be overwhelming. Therefore, I've distilled everything down into easy-to-understand concepts. After you're done reading and you've begun writing, watch the videos in the Resources section to help you dig deeper if you get stuck.

· · ·

FINAL NOTE

This book contains affiliate links to products or services that I recommend and use myself. If you purchase through these links, I receive a small commission at no extra cost to you. You are under no obligation to buy through my links, but thank you if you do!

FREQUENTLY ASKED QUESTIONS ABOUT WRITING A NOVEL

I'm sure there are many, many questions floating around in your head about exactly how you're going to write a novel.

After all, it's not an easy undertaking. You probably have a significant other, a family, a job, and other things that require your daily attention.

Maybe you've never written anything before.

Trust me, I know it seems impossible. But writers do it every day.

Let's go over the top most frequently asked questions about this topic so that we can overcome any barriers you may still have. By the end of this section, you'll have all the mental fortitude you'll need to write your book.

HOW CAN I POSSIBLY EVER WRITE A NOVEL?

I've studied a lot of working writers over the years (it's what I do), and they're all different. But the successful ones usually have a combination of things:

- They have **time management**, because they're often writing "in the cracks of life"—between work, family, school, and other hobbies. Writing takes a significant amount of time, and in order to do it, these writers must make hard decisions on how to balance all the elements of their life, and they must also make some sacrifices.
- They have **discipline** to show up every day and write the words, even when they don't want to.
- They have **a higher purpose** that drives them beyond simply wanting to write a novel. Some want to build a career from their books and write full-time because they hate their jobs. Others write to engage with the community of readers who gather around their books. Others, like me, write simply because it connects them with their passion and

they want nothing in return—just the fact that someone, somewhere enjoyed it.

Contrary to popular belief, you don't need confidence or experience.

Trust me when I say that there are Amazon and *New York Times* Bestsellers who are complete Eeyores behind closed doors. They need others to validate them, even though they're successful. There are, also, writers who can't sell a single book who are the most confident people you will ever meet, sometimes annoyingly so.

I don't want you to think that confidence isn't important. It is immensely important. But you can build your confidence as you go, and finishing your first novel is a tremendous way to boost it. Once you've done this, your idea of what is possible will change.

As for experience, you don't need to have written a bunch of novels in order to do this. Believe it or not, less experience is better. You don't have any bad habits. As you'll discover in this book, bad habits and reliance on writing myths are more responsible for failed writers than anything else.

Remember: you just need strong time management, discipline, and a higher purpose.

You should already know what the higher purpose is. What's your "why?" In other words, you're a writer because...?

Make sure you're clear on that.

HOW DO I WRITE A NOVEL WITHOUT GOING CRAZY?

FIRST, have a talk with your significant other or spouse. Writing a novel is impossible without their support. They're going to be tending to other matters while you're writing, such as cooking, cleaning, taking care of the kids, etc.

Make sure they understand what you're doing and how important it is to you. Make sure that you're giving them the support they need when you aren't writing.

It's hard to have a writing career without your significant other behind you, and charging onward without their help is not something I recommend.

Second, your health is not worth jeopardizing for this. It's easy to skip nutritious meals, sleep less, and do irreparable damage to your body by trying to sprint to the end of your novel. Not worth it. All of the techniques I recommend in this book are healthy, but I recommend that you think about how you can keep healthy. That includes a proper diet, exercise, and time to de-stress.

Third, I don't recommend that you "reward" yourself for milestones. A lot of people will say, "If I can write 10,000 words, I'll do something special for myself."

If you want to reward yourself for finishing your book, that's fine.

But do not reward yourself before then.

Writing must be its own reward. That's a secret mindset that professional writers (those making a living from their writing) have adopted. Treat it as such.

So yes, you can absolutely do this without going crazy.

If you're still feeling anxious about how you're going to do this, consider these facts:

- Somewhere, right now, at this very moment, someone is writing a novel. They might be a little stressed, but they're not going crazy.
- Somewhere, right now, at this very moment, someone is writing the final sentence in their novel. They are probably feeling super excited.
- Somewhere, right now, a reader is finding a new book for the first time, and it will bring them joy and delight.

So keep it in perspective. Writers do this every second of every day, and last I heard, no one lost their minds writing a novel, even though the process might have been maddening for them at times. When you write your novel, you're joining in the collective consciousness of every writer who's ever existed. You're a part of something special, and it's an exclusive club. It will be overwhelming at times, but I'll help you through it.

Heck, I've written 40 books and I still have all my hair!

Trust me when I say you can do this, and by the time you're done reading this book, you're going to be pumped about getting started.

HOW DO I FIND TIME TO WRITE WHEN I HAVE A FULL-TIME JOB / FAMILY / ETC.?

I WANT you to make a list of everything in your life that demands attention.

Decide what you're going to START, STOP, and CONTINUE.

You may not want to hear this, but you have to be ruthless with your time.

Let me give you some examples of things I chose to stop:

- I love video games, but I decided that my writing career is more important.
- I love music. In fact, I play several instruments and used to write music. But my songwriting was going nowhere, so I quit composing, and I sold all of my instruments to fund my first few books.
- I don't watch movies or television anymore, except in limited sessions with my wife and daughter. If I have downtime, I do NOT watch television.
- I used to attend local writing groups in my city. I stopped attending those.

- I cut back considerably on socializing on the weekends.
- I've passed on job promotions because they would have disrupted my work/life balance.
- I've quit friendships that did not support my writing habit.

You don't have to be as austere as I am, but I encourage you to think about what you're going to start, stop, and continue during the time you'll be writing.

I don't watch television much anymore, but I read like crazy because it's important to consume content. I just choose how I consume my content carefully and purposefully. Maybe television and movies motivate you and inspire you to write; you just need to be cognizant of the time you spend watching them.

There are only so many hours in the day, and you can only split your focus so much.

WHERE DO I COME UP WITH STORY IDEAS?

Almost no writer I know has trouble coming up with ideas; it's usually the opposite.

If your mind is empty and you can't find what to write, consider the following:

- How much fiction are you reading? A lack of ideas usually stems from lack of exposing yourself to stories. Expose yourself to more stories and this should fix the problem.
- What genres are you passionate about? Could it be that you're wanting to write, say, a science fiction story when maybe fantasy is a better fit for you?
- Think about the books that resonated with you most as a reader. Now think about the bigger archetypes behind those novels. What speaks to you? "Chosen one" stories? Underdogs? Redemption stories? Origin stories? Pick one that you're passionate about, then pick a genre. Try to write that kind of story. Sometimes thinking about this at the macro level is enough to give you some ideas.

Another tip I recommend is to keep a sketchbook or diary of ideas. You can do this via a notebook or an app like Evernote or Microsoft OneNote. Any time you come up with an interesting idea, make a habit of writing it down. If you do this over time, you'll have more ideas than you know what to do with.

I've kept a sketchbook since high school, and I have thousands of ideas, big and small. Any time I'm struggling to find something to write, I browse through my entries. It works really well, and it's one of the secrets to my creativity.

Now is a fantastic time to commit to starting a sketchbook because when you're writing your novel, you're going to be very inspired. Once you get into a state of flow, you'll find that fun book ideas may come to you randomly. Capture them.

HOW DO I TURN MY IDEAS INTO A STORY?

Let's keep it simple.

I want you to think about the following framework. It will help you realize what you already know, focus on what to work on, and guide you when you get stuck. I call it the Writer's Rule of Thirds.

STORY RULE #1: YOUR BOOK HAS THREE PARTS

First, let's talk about story and the Three-Act Structure.

I guarantee you know this already.

Act One: Setup. Reader meets the hero and the stakes are introduced.

Act Two: Confrontation. The stakes rise, the hero experiences a string of successes and setbacks against the villain.

Act Three: Resolution. Tension reaches its highest level. Final battle with the villain, tension reduced, loose ends tied up (or not).

To keep this simple, the Three-Act Structure is really just a beginning, middle, and end. Every story has a beginning, middle, and end, right?

STORY RULE #2: EVERY CHAPTER IN YOUR BOOK HAS THREE PARTS

Just as your story has a beginning, middle, and end, so do your chapters. Every chapter has setup, conflict, and resolution. The resolution is usually a cliffhanger that makes the reader want to turn the page.

STORY RULE #3: EVERY SECTION IN YOUR CHAPTERS HAS 3 BUILDING BLOCKS

Quick exercise: grab any commercial fiction novel (written within the last fifty years) and turn to a random page. On any page, there are three elements working in tandem to comprise the story: dialogue, narrative, and action (let's call it DNA for short).

Dialogue consists of three parts: quotation marks, the words being said, and a tag, such as "he said." That's it.

Narrative is more expansive. For example, the narrator may be telling the reader about something, such as the background of a place, summarizing an event, or details about another character (known as exposition). When this happens too frequently, readers may accuse the writer of "telling" and not "showing."

When it happens too little, readers may say that the book moved too fast or lacked character development.

Action is action: characters in movement, propelling the story itself forward. Lots of action verbs. Action differs from narrative because it advances the story, whereas narrative slows it down.

If you think about DNA as Legos, you can snap them together to "build" your story. If you and I were to build Lego castle, yours would look different than mine, but the building blocks would be the same. Stories are the same way. Every writer builds their stories differently, but the underlying blocks are the same. This is why you can open up a Stephen King novel and see pages and pages of narrative, or a James Patterson novel, where you'll see a mix of all three elements—switching almost like clockwork—or a Nora Roberts novel, where dialogue is the star, especially when the romance is growing.

There is no right or wrong way. Just your way.

We could also talk about point of view, pacing, character development, and other elements of story that you've no doubt heard of, but really, those elements are dependent on how you put your DNA together.

Just remember the Writer's Rule of Thirds: your book has three parts, every chapter in your book has three parts, and every section in your chapter has three elements: dialogue, narrative, and action.

Understand that framework, and suddenly your story ideas will have a dependable, reliable structure that you can follow from start to finish, even if you don't know what to write.

WHAT IF I FAIL?

You only fail if you give up.

Consider this: many people "say" they want to write a book but never get around to it; fewer people start writing a book but never finish it; even fewer publish their finished book; the fewest of all build a writing career from those books.

Writers generally aren't number people. Numbers are sad.

So don't be a statistic. Be a success story.

If it helps you to get an accountability partner, do it. Do whatever you have to do to get the words on the page. Your career depends on it. Even if it's a couple hundred words, you can build a long-term writing career with that as long as you have consistency and momentum.

You cannot build a writing career from nothing.

And you probably noticed that I'm talking about a writing career here. (But, Michael, I just want to write a novel!)

Sorry, I am going to ask you to think bigger. If you're just wanting to write that one book to cross it off your bucket list before you die, that's totally fine. You have permission to ignore the rest of this chapter. But I'm 99% sure you're not that kind of writer.

I suspect you want more from your writing than just finishing your first book. You probably want to live the dream of being a successful writer. Right? Right?

Whether you like it or not, the rest of your life depends on what you do today.

Do. And do well.

It's not just enough to start. You must learn to start and finish. That's how you build a career.

Remember: you only fail if you give up. Don't give up, and you won't fail.

I know, I know: it's so basic. I'm just delivering a dose of ass-kicking now because you're going to need it ten to fifteen days into your book when the "honeymoon" has ended and you start second-guessing your commitment.

HOW LONG SHOULD MY NOVEL BE? WHAT IF MY NOVEL IS TOO SHORT / LONG?

I HEAR this question all the time. Writers have so many myths in their heads about how long a story should be.

My advice: focus on the story, not the length. If the story decides it wants to be 49,000 words, you need to be okay with that. If it decides it wants to be 100,000 words, then you need to be okay with that too.

Here's the thing about book length: despite what people say (and everyone has an opinion about this), there are no rules.

Readers don't say, "I'm giving this book one star because it wasn't 50,000 words," or "I only buy books that are 100,000 words or more."

Length has little importance in a reader's buying decision, but it does have major importance in their reviews.

Readers will call out a "padded" story every time. No one likes subplots that were added for no reason, or pages full of exposition that have no purpose.

So please. If you write a 40,000-word novel, resist the urge to add more to get it to 50,000. While some readers may quibble with whether your book is a "novel," they likely won't quibble with the story itself.

I, too, struggled with the "length" myth for a long time, it was the hardest for me to dispel. It's hard, but you have to do it because it's perpetuated by writers, not readers.

No one wants to live in a world where every book is the same length. What if Tolkien cut his Lord of the Rings books down to 50,000 words? Or what if Hemingway doubled the size of *The Old Man and the Sea* in order to satisfy the 50,000-word "rule"? That would be sad.

WHAT IF I DON'T KNOW ANYTHING ABOUT THE WRITING CRAFT?

Have you read a novel?

If so, then you do know something about the writing craft. You may not know how to articulate it, but the very act of reading teaches you about writing craft.

My goal in this book is to teach you how to recognize the most important elements of fiction so that you can learn to master them.

So the short answer is to keep reading.

The long answer is this book itself.

Don't worry about not being an expert at the craft—that takes a lifetime. All you need to get started is a desire to write. Let this book be your guide.

BEFORE YOU WRITE: TOOLS YOU'LL NEED

Just as a carpenter needs tools, so does a writer.

I believe that your writing app is the most important investment you can ever make in your career. Nothing comes above it.

Imagine Tiger Woods winning the PGA Tour with a set of golf clubs he bought on Amazon...or Annie Leibovitz doing a magazine cover photo shoot with a camera she bought at a thrift store...Funny, right?

The tool makes the writer.

Another story. When I was in fifth grade, I tried out for band. I loved the idea of playing an instrument and performing for people.

I'll never forget the audition. After school on a Monday night, my mom and I walked into a stuffy band room with no windows. Shiny trumpets and baritones hung on the walls, and the room had a worn, metallic, carpety smell that only band rooms have.

The band teacher, a middle-aged woman wearing a business

blouse and jeans, lined me up with a bunch of other kids, and she studied us, stared at us intensely as she walked the line. As a fifth grader, I had never been more intimidated in my life.

She asked us questions. She asked the parents questions. I don't think we even touched an instrument during the audition. But there were instruments on display, and somehow at the end of it, I was accepted into the Kirby Middle School Junior Band as an alto saxophone player.

My band teacher told my mom something that has always stuck with me: "The child doesn't choose the instrument. The instrument chooses the child."

The saxophone chose me.

As I learned how to play it, it became an extension of my arms and fingers. It sounds cheesy, but there were many times when I was "one" with my sax, particularly later in life when I played jazz. I treated it with the utmost respect.

And, I've always gotten along with other saxophone players. My best friend played the sax. I meet random people at events, and after long conversations, it often comes out that we played the saxophone in school. Sax people are weird like that, and we gravitate toward each other.

But back to writing.

Just like a professional saxophone player's livelihood depends on the quality and knowledge of his or her instrument, your writing career depends on the quality and knowledge of whatever app you choose to write with.

It also opens the door to build relationships with other writers who use the same app, so that you can learn from each other and "talk shop." Choosing a good app will help you bond with other writers.

I ask you to choose a writing app, but what I really mean is that you need to put yourself in a position for your "perfect" writing app to choose you.

Ladies and gentlemen, in this chapter, I present to you the best writing apps on the market today!
"Choose" wisely...

MICROSOFT WORD: THE APP FOR TRADITIONALISTS

SOME PEOPLE MAY BE SURPRISED to see Microsoft Word on this list, but the truth is that for all its failings, it is a solid writing app. If you own a Windows computer, you already have it.

The DOCX format is universal, and when you're ready to publish your book, almost all of the major ebook retailers will accept a DOCX file.

Word is also the most commonly used program to prepare paperback files.

It is also the program of choice for most editors, and they make extensive use of the Track Changes feature to provide edits.

Overall, Word is a common language that almost everyone speaks. Even if you don't use Word for writing, chances are high that you will need it for one reason or another.

Word is for you if you prefer convenience and a familiar way of doing things.

However, that convenience and familiarity come at a price.

Keeping your novel in one file is unwieldy, even with a table of contents.

Backing up Microsoft Word files can be an exercise in frustration, and it's easy to lose data, even if you're careful.

If you use Word, you're also stuck in Microsoft's ecosystem. As far as I know, Microsoft has no plans to make author-centric updates to the app.

But if you choose Word and are prepared to learn its quirks, I highly recommend taking an online Microsoft Word course. Sites like Udemy or Lynda provide affordable courses that will help you improve your skill level. If you choose not to take a course, be prepared to spend hours diagnosing problems down the road, especially if you plan to use Word for paperback formatting. I'm not kidding.

And for Apple users, Pages is an acceptable Word alternative, though it doesn't have all of Word's features.

ULYSSES: THE WRITING APP FOR WRITERS WHO NEED SIMPLICITY

Microsoft Word and Ulysses could not be any more different.

Word is linear. Ulysses is expansive.

Word is boring. Ulysses is beautiful.

Word is a standard word processor. Ulysses uses a syntax called Markdown, and if you've never seen Markdown with its hashtags and brackets, it makes the app look instantly more modern and understated.

Unlike Word, Ulysses is a writing app designed specifically for writers. I can only use two words to describe it: elegant and beautiful. It's for writers who like simplicity with tons of features under the hood.

It uses a universal library, so instead of individual files, everything you write is stored in the library, accessible at any time with one click. The app is blazing fast.

Ulysses also utilizes a folder system on the left-hand side, so you can split up your chapters and access them easily. You can also tag your chapters with keywords.

The app can also display your word counts and help you set writing goals.

It has a white and a dark mode if you're into that, and it exports beautiful ebooks with just one click.

It also has a full-featured iOS app that syncs your work between as many devices as you want.

In my opinion, Ulysses is a viable alternative to Word.

The biggest thing to get used to is Markdown—it's a syntax that was designed to convert easily to HTML. This means that your files are slim and have little fat, unlike Word docs. As much as I like it, Markdown is not for everyone.

I use Ulysses daily for blogging and my YouTube video scripts, but I've also written novels in it, so I can highly recommend it if you are interested.

Ulysses is the app for writers who dare to be different. It is currently Mac-only and you have to pay for a subscription (40 dollars per year), but the cost is worth it.

For more information on Ulysses, watch my Ulysses Essentials video series on YouTube, where I review the app and show it in action.

SCRIVENER: THE CAVIAR OF WRITING APPS

BASED on the title of this section, you already know which app I use!

If you haven't heard of it, Scrivener is an app from Literature & Latte that focuses solely on the author experience.

I call Scrivener the "caviar of writing apps" for good reason. Every feature was designed with authors in mind.

Scrivener takes the standard word processor engine of Word and combines it with features that authors need.

Instead of the linear, up-down experience that you get with Word, Scrivener has a binder on the left side of the screen that allows you to jump easily between chapters. The binder also stores your research and any notes you make, and it won't include those when it's time to export your book. That means you can store your outline, research, and your novel cleanly in the same file, and click between them effortlessly.

You can create split screens, with your outline on one half of the screen and your novel on the other half.

You can track revisions in Scrivener's Revision Mode, and it will color code each of your drafts.

You can write on your Mac, on your iPad, on your iPhone, and sync between your devices with one touch.

You can write in full-screen mode.

You can track your word counts and set daily goals.

I could go on, but do you see why I love Scrivener so much?

Scrivener is not just a solid writing app—it's an amazing app with tons of bells and whistles.

At just 45 dollars (at the time of this writing), it is an incredible investment.

STORY TIME

I bought Scrivener in 2010. I was fed up with Word, and I was desperate for anything different.

I found Scrivener and instantly knew it was the app for me. However...the app cost 35 dollars at the time and I didn't have the money.

I was a college grad, I was broke, I had crazy student loans, and I barely had three dollars, let alone 35. And, to make things worse, I had to upgrade my computer in order to run Scrivener.

So that 35 dollars was actually around three hundred...

I sold some of my musical instruments. I worked overtime in a crappy desk job. I cut back on virtually all of my expenses in order to afford Scrivener.

To this date, that sacrifice was the best investment I ever made.

For the first time in my writing career, I could finally get out of my own way and just focus on the words. Scrivener not only made writing easy—it made it fun and consistent. There's a lot to be said about a stable, reliable writing app that's always there for you, with features that come in handy when you need them.

This chapter can't do Scrivener justice, so watch my YouTube playlist called Scrivener Essentials. I go through everything you need to know, and I showcase why Scrivener is so special.

SPELLING AND GRAMMAR CHECKERS: SILENT PARTNERS IN YOUR NOVEL WRITING PROCESS

Let's face it: Microsoft Word's spell checker isn't good enough.

Fortunately, technology has come a long way, and there are a number of spelling and grammar checkers on the market that are more accurate than Word.

The two that I recommend are Grammarly and ProWriting-Aid. Grammarly is geared toward a general audience, and ProWritingAid is geared specifically toward fiction writers.

The nice thing about each of these apps is that they will catch a handful of pesky spelling and grammar errors that you missed.

Both Grammarly and ProWritingAid have browser versions, browser extensions, desktop apps, and mobile support so you can take them with you. They also provide the added benefit of sitting on top of any text field in your browser and emails, silently checking your work in the background as you type.

Both apps have fully-functional free versions with only a few limitations so you can give them a try first.

Check out my video reviews on Grammarly and ProWritingAid as well as an epic app battle video where I compare the two.

NOTE-TAKING APPS: ALL YOUR RESEARCH AT YOUR DISPOSAL

A NOTE-TAKING app lets you store research and other notes that might be relevant to your novel.

If you use an app like Scrivener or Ulysses, you don't need one. If you use Word, you do.

The most popular note-taking app is Evernote. It's a digital notebook that lets you capture notes so you can refer to them later. You can add photos, audio, and even sketches. The browser extension, the Evernote Web Clipper, lets you capture pages off the Internet and include them in your notebook.

Evernote is an invaluable tool that can help you stay organized. Best of all, the free version should satisfy most people's needs.

There are also Evernote alternatives such as Microsoft OneNote, Google Keep, and Bear. Find the one that works best for you.

FINAL CONSIDERATIONS

We've covered the best three writing apps on the market, two good spelling and grammar checking apps, and the best note-taking apps.

That's all you need for now. Honestly, the spelling and grammar checker and note-taking apps are optional.

If you still need some help in deciding which writing app you should use, here are my recommendations.

If you are old-school or prefer what you know, use Microsoft Word (or Pages for Mac). You can get started right away and learn what you need to learn when you need to learn it.

If you want the best of the best, with every bell and whistle imaginable, then use Scrivener.

If you want to focus on simply getting the words down, and you don't need fancy stuff, then use Ulysses. It has the best of Scrivener and Word while also offering a zippier experience.

PLANNING YOUR NOVEL

Let's help you get ready to write your novel.

Fair warning that the items in this chapter can easily turn into time sucks if you let them. That's why, if possible, I recommend that you don't spend too much time prepping to write your novel.

Writers write. If you spend all your time planning, you may not ever get around to writing.

Move purposefully through this section so that you can start writing as soon as possible.

Not every novel needs research, but if yours does, now is the time to do it.

In the 30+ novels I've written, I've needed to do some kind of research on at least 25 of them.

Research is important, because if you don't get certain facts right, readers will either stop reading or they'll call you out on it.

Research tends to paralyze writers because they don't know when to stop. There are blog posts and podcasts out there that recommend extensive research templates, with world-building checklists that are sometimes many pages long.

That's garbage.

I believe in practicality. Here's what you need to know: there are two types of research that you can do.

METHOD #1: FOUNDATIONAL RESEARCH

This is the research you need to do before you can even start writing.

For example, if you want to write a Regency romance, but you know nothing about England during the British Regency, you would need to spend some time understanding how people spoke, how they dressed, what everyday life was like, etc. Otherwise, you'll write a novel with incorrect factual and historical details.

If you want to write a hardboiled detective novel that takes place in your hometown, that might be easier. Assuming you don't need to do much research on your town, you would just need to make sure you're getting the police procedure right.

If you want to write a science fiction novel about artificial intelligence, you would need to read up on current theories and philosophies about the future of AI so that your technology is plausible.

I had to do a significant amount of foundational research for my science fiction series, Android X. It takes place in the year 2300, where androids and humans live together in peace after a devastating singularity. During my foundational research, I had to understand the following areas before I could start writing:

- Artificial intelligence: how it works, projections from experts on what it would look like in one hundred to two hundred years. In other words, what do scientists think androids will be able to do, and are there limits?
- Futurism: how would I project the future so that it feels plausible?
- World governments: My story involves a universal world government, so how could something like that happen and exist in my story without readers rolling their eyes?
- Technology: What kind of technology would exist

in the year 2300 and how would it shape people's everyday lives?

Here's a combination of what most writers do: they spend hours on Google, Wikipedia, and YouTube, go to the library and check out a dozen books, interview people, read all the books in their genre, buy nonfiction books on the topic, listen to podcasts on the topic, and scour any resource they can to learn about the potential world they want to create.

Any of those topics by themselves are fine, but where writers go wrong is that they believe that they need to do them all.

I know writers who spend months researching. If that's you, then you're doing it wrong (unless you're writing in a genre that requires extensive research, like historical fiction or very hard science fiction).

Foundational research is like a gate. If the gate is closed, you can't go through it. But once it's open, you can proceed. Fortunately for you, the gate always opens sooner than you think.

The key is knowing when the gate is open. Many writers only need a little bit to begin their journey, yet they keep researching, even though the gate is wide open and swinging in the wind.

For my Android X series, I did three simple things that helped me create a plausible futuristic world and characters in less than two weeks.

1. I read two layperson-centric books by experts: *The Physics of the Future* by Michio Kaku and *Think Like a Futurist* by Cecily Sommers. I read them simply to understand the broader concepts of what two experts in their fields think about the next couple hundred years. I kept the focus of my novel

within the philosophical constraints of these two books. This way, I didn't have to worry about doing too much additional research and it gave the technology and society a cohesive theme.

2. I watched an hour's worth of YouTube videos of relevant videos.

3. I found a long-form blog post on a magazine website that explored virtual reality.

After that, the gate opened.

It's true that I still didn't understand all the intricate details I would have needed to know. It's also true that I still had research left to do.

But the foundational research helped me understand the basics so I could get started. In the reviews for *Android Paradox*, Book 1 in my Android X series, readers said they enjoyed the futuristic setting. Very few quibbled with the science.

That's what foundational research does. It creates the foundation for plausibility—nothing more, nothing less.

METHOD #2: JUST-IN-TIME RESEARCH

Once you've made it through the gate, your writing journey begins. There will be many times throughout writing the book that you'll need to stop and do research.

That's where just-in-time research comes in. You research topics as they come up.

This is better because it's easy to spend weeks researching something, only not to need it in your book. Writers do one of two things when this happens: they either feel defeated because they wasted time, or they try to find ways to cram all their research into the novel ("I spent all this time reading those history books, damn it, and I'm not going to waste it!")

Just-in-time eliminates this risk entirely, ensuring that you only research the items that will actually end up in your book.

Most of your research should be just-in-time research. This will help keep you producing words every day, with interruptions here and there as needed.

Just-in-time research is like a speed bump. It slows you down, but just for a few seconds. Go too fast over it, though, and you'll mess up your shocks.

To give another example from my Android X series, there's a chapter in the book where one of the protagonists visits an attorney's office. I've been to many law offices in my life, but I had to think hard about what one would look like in the year 2300. So I had to take a few minutes to do some Google research on what law offices look like today, and then do some brainstorming on what would change. First, there wouldn't be any books or bookshelves, which are an iconic symbol of law offices today. After a bit of brainstorming, I decided that law offices probably wouldn't even exist. Artificial intelligence would eliminate the need for receptionists, paralegals, and lawyers, replacing them with algorithms that instead would advocate for clients based on factual details. So I came up with the idea that people in the future would visit "virtual" law offices in the year 2300, and instead of interacting with real attorneys, they would interact with "robo attorneys" who looked human but were really just avatars of a hyper-advanced algorithm. The few human attorneys that did exist would handle only unique cases and function more like engineers of their firms' algorithms.

About 30 minutes later, I was writing again. That's a good example of just-in-time research. I don't outline, so I would have never thought to research a futuristic law office before writing the series.

I'll bet that if I added up all the time I spent doing just-in-time research throughout the course of a novel, it would equal several hours, maybe more. It's still research, but it's directed and intentional.

THE POWER OF ANCHOR CONTENT

If you wanted, you could read the works of every expert in the subject matter areas of your book. Some writers do that, but you and I can agree that that's too time-consuming. Right? Right?

Instead, consider what I call "anchor content." Anchor content is content that by itself forms the foundation of your foundational research. It should be the first place you consult whenever you do just-in-time research. For my Android X series, my anchor content was the two books I mentioned by Michio Kaku and Cecily Sommers.

Whenever I had a situation of just-in-time research, I consulted those books first to see if they commented on what I needed. Most of the time, there was something there that I could use as a starting point for a brainstorm session without having to do additional research. If the books were silent, I looked outside of them for guidance. In other words, the anchor content "anchored" me from doing extraneous research.

Another benefit of anchor content is that if you pick the right content, it helps you create a unified theme in your story. For example, I'm a big fan of Michio Kaku, and I like to think that he and I share the same outlook for the future. As a result, my series is quite positive in how it treats android technology and artificial intelligence. A lot of Kaku's concepts informed the way I think about the future, and so you'll find them pop up now and again in my book—mixed in with my own philosophies, of course.

This is why I'm an advocate of finding popular nonfiction books as a starting point for your research wherever possible. They help you think bigger and broader and eliminate a lot of manual work on your part.

Popular nonfiction means books by authors like Bill Bryson, Daniel Pink, Malcolm Gladwell, etc. They're often extremely focused on one or two concepts, targeted at a broad audience.

Popular nonfiction is often written in an easy-to-understand style, and the authors break concepts down so that everyday people can understand them and use them to improve their lives. Another benefit of popular nonfiction is that it's usually available in ebook and audiobook format, which helps you consume it faster.

Yet another benefit of popular nonfiction is that despite its simple approach, it is thoroughly researched, so much of the difficult stuff has already been done for you. All you have to do is find the right book. Most of them also include references and sources, so if there was ever a concept you wanted to explore further, you could use those as a jumping-off point.

In other words, popular nonfiction makes great anchor content and can save you time and effort, thus allowing you to focus on writing.

Remember too that every novel is different and requires different research demands. Maybe the anchor content you need isn't a book. Maybe it's a series of TED Talks, or YouTube videos, or a documentary. Do what works for you.

HOW DETAILED SHOULD YOUR NOTES BE?

. . .

If you take notes, they should be detailed enough to help you remember what you researched so that you can incorporate it into your book later.

Here are some other things to consider when taking your notes:

- Always be asking "what if" when you're researching. It's the sole question that will help you find the info you need and also fuel your creativity.
- See a scene, person, place, or thing that you want to put in your story? When you encounter it, capture it in the five senses. What does it look, smell, feel, taste, and sound like? Capturing it in five dimensions now will make it super easy to import it into your story later, especially when you're in the murky middle of your novel and your brain isn't working.

MY STEP-BY-STEP GUIDE TO RESEARCH

Here's a series of steps to ensure that you don't get bogged down by research.

Foundational Research

1. Map out 1-2 subject areas that you need to understand in order to start writing. Spend no more than 30 minutes on this.
2. Figure out who the pre-eminent experts are for each

of those subject areas. Pick 1 expert per subject area.

3. Buy/borrow 1 key book from those experts and find your anchor content. If those experts happen to have podcast interviews, blog articles, YouTube videos or TED Talks, allow yourself up to 2 hours consuming their content in addition to reading their books. If you don't like the content, find another expert.

4. Determine how long it will take you to get through the material. Every novel is different, but remember: writers write, instead of spending all their time researching. Set a hard deadline.

5. Consume the content quickly, taking detailed but not extensive notes.

6. Beat your deadline. Then, start writing.

Just-in-Time Research

1. Write your novel.

2. Whenever you come across something you're not sure about in your story, consult your anchor content first. If you cannot find what you need in your anchor content, branch out and do more research, but set a timer and don't allow yourself to spend too much time researching. Find what you need, make absolute sure that you understand it, take quick notes, and get back to writing as soon as possible.

3. Rinse and repeat.

OUTLINING

THE NEXT DECISION you need to make is whether you are going to outline.

Knowing how to write a novel with an outline is a valuable skill. So is knowing how to write a novel without an outline.

For the sake of your first novel, I want you to choose one and commit to it. You can always change your style later.

Outlining serves one purpose: to plan your story so you always know what to write. When done correctly, it's a safeguard against writer's block and it will help you stay focused.

However, in my experience, I have found that outlining also has three negative consequences that almost no one talks about, probably because it is such a commonly-accepted best practice that few are willing to look past its flaws.

The first negative consequence of outlining is that it's a graveyard for aspiring writers. Many people never make it past this phase. The act paralyzes them, intimidates them, or both.

The second negative consequence of outlining is that it's not always going to be accurate. Often, your story will veer away from what you planned. It happens, trust me.

The third negative consequence of outlining is that when your story changes direction, it creates a paradox.

This is a bigger problem than you might think. Should you force yourself to follow your outline, or should you follow your instinct? If you stick to your outline, you'll ignore your muse, which is a big no-no, especially when you consider that your instinct is almost always correct (remember what your parents told you!). If you follow your instinct, though, you'll throw the time and effort that you spent on your outline into the trash, which is defeating.

After all, if you spend several hours creating an outline, it's going to feel like you wasted your time when you don't use that material. That creates doubt, and doubt leads to fear, and fear leads to writer's block.

In a later book in this series, *Be a Writing Machine*, I share some stronger opinions against outlining and why I think you should ultimately ditch it, but that's too advanced for most beginners and if you've never written a novel before, you're not ready for that.

For the sake of this book, I am including outlining as a viable option. I will, however, share some perspectives to help you think about it differently so that you can get the most value out of it.

Here's the decision you need to make.

If you're going to outline, decide if you're okay with wasting outline material. If you are, then treat your outline as nothing more than a tool to help you begin your story. Think of it as training wheels on a bike; they serve their purpose, but when you take them off, you don't need them anymore. When your story inevitably changes direction, follow the story and ditch the outline.

If you're not okay with ignoring your outline material (many writers aren't), then commit to spending less time on your outline. Namely, do not outline your book chapter-by-chapter. Instead, follow a broad outlining method like The Hero's Journey, or simply map out a few key scenes that you know will happen, and then leave the rest to be filled in later as you write. This way, those key scenes will be your guideposts; you just have to get to them. The risk of writer's block is higher, but I've got plenty of bulletproof tools later in this book to help you with that.

A STORY ABOUT CHAPTER-BY-CHAPTER OUTLINING

With my novel, *Theo and the Festival of Shadows,* I laboriously mapped out every chapter. Before I started writing, I knew exactly what was going to happen in every chapter. The novel is interactive and styled after *Choose Your Own Adventures,* so it has several different plots and subplots, depending on what the reader chooses, making it even more complicated to outline. But I figured it out and developed an outline that I was proud of.

Around chapter three, the story decided it wanted to go a different direction.

It sucked. I was angry about my outline being wrong, yet I knew in my heart that I had to let the story work itself out.

I trusted my instinct. When I finished the novel, the end result barely resembled the outline. However, the major scenes were relatively intact.

I realized something very important: whenever the story decided it wanted to go in a different direction, it happened at the chapter level. The work I did in the individual scenes almost always changed in some way. I changed character names. I added or deleted characters from scenes. I deleted some scenes entirely because they didn't add any value to the story.

I learned to not outline the little details like that since they were going to change anyway.

I suspect this will be true for you if you outline, so learn from my mistake. This is why I do not recommend chapter-by-chapter outlining if you are not okay with deviating from your outline.

HOW TO OUTLINE CORRECTLY

This chapter will briefly cover the major outlining methods, as well as some tips on how to write your novel without an outline if that's your preference.

Full disclosure: I no longer outline my novels, and haven't done so since novel ten or so. But outlining did help me early in my career. I've used all of the major outlining methods and know them well enough to teach them.

There are many outlining methods, and every few years, it seems like a new one appears. I've seen and used most of them, and I've included the most effective ones in this chapter.

Use this chapter as a starting point for understanding the major outlining methods.

Be sure to check the Resources section for links to all the books mentioned in this chapter.

HERO'S JOURNEY

. . .

This is perhaps the most popular outlining method, made famous by Joseph Campbell's *The Hero with A Thousand Faces*.

The Hero's Journey is a wheel with the following points:

- **Call to adventure**: Hero is comfortable in the only world they've ever known.
- **Supernatural aid**: In the face of trouble, something saves the hero and exposes them to the unknown.
- **Threshold**: Hero crosses the threshold from known into unknown.
- **Challenges**: Hero faces challenges and setbacks, receiving help from mentors along the way (like Luke Skywalker in *Star Wars*).
- **Abyss**: The hero faces his or her darkest moment but rises from it with renewed strength.
- **Transformation and atonement**: Hero undergoes a major transformation and atonement to win the final battle with the villain.
- **Return**: Hero returns home victorious and more complete than when they left.

I've simplified the steps, but those are the key elements.

The advantage of the Hero's Journey is that it's popular, so readers are familiar with it. Almost every iconic pop culture action movie follows it.

The disadvantage of the Hero's Journey is that it can feel too formulaic and predictable at times because it is so common. Also, not all heroes have mentors as Luke Skywalker did with Obi-Wan Kenobi, so if your hero doesn't have a mentor and you use the Hero's Journey, it will feel like something is missing.

The Hero's Journey doesn't (quite) work with antiheroes either.

THREE-ACT STRUCTURE

Every story has a beginning, middle, and end—three acts. This method was popularized by plays, which are commonly broken into acts.

The advantage of the three-act structure is that you only need a basic understanding of your beginning, middle, and end. In many ways, it's the simplest and purest of all the methods in this chapter.

The disadvantage of this method is that there's no structure. If you've never written a novel before, you will probably find this method lacking. If you're a first-time writer and this method resonates with you, I recommend that you pair it with another more structured method, like The Hero's Journey or the Plot Point Method.

PLOT POINT METHOD

The plot point method got its start with screenplays. Syd Field popularized it with his book, *Screenplay*, and Larry Brooks adapted it for novelists with his book, *Story Engineering*.

Perhaps the most structured of all the methods in this chapter, the allure of the plot point method is that it tells you exactly what needs to happen in your story and when. This is a necessity with screenplays that translates nicely to commercial genre fiction novels.

I used the plot point method for my first few novels, and it is the method that made outlining "click" for me.

Here are the plot points.

- **Inciting Incident**: Hero faces a conflict that begins the story.
- **Plot Point 1:** The point of no return. The hero has no choice but to embark on the quest.
- **Pinch Point 1**: Villain appears or creates a setback for the hero.
- **Midpoint (also known as Plot Point 2)**: The point where things change in the hero's favor, usually through a turn of events or a piece of information that gives the hero power. The hero transitions from being reactive to proactive.
- **Pinch Point 2**: Another setback from the villain.
- **Plot Point 3**: Calm before the storm. Hero gears up for the final battle.
- **Black Moment**: The worst happens to the hero and all seems lost.
- **Final Battle (also known as Climax)**: Showdown with the villain; hero is triumphant.
- **Resolution**: Story ends with any remaining threads tied up.

The advantage of using the plot point method is that it gives you a solid structure. Like the Hero's Journey, the plot point method is also prevalent in movies, so it's easy to learn and replicate.

The disadvantage of this method is that if you're not careful, you'll end up with a super short novel. This method was created with screenplays in mind, and writers often struggle to adapt it for novels. They move from plot point to plot point without letting the story breathe. The method doesn't account for subplots or deep character development either, which only exacerbates the problem.

If you're going to use this method, determine how you're going to build in subplots, character development, and additional meat to the story.

MIRROR MOMENT

The term "mirror moment" was coined by James Scott Bell in his book *Write Your Book from the Middle*.

It refers to a single moment in the middle of the novel when the hero sees themselves in a proverbial mirror, realizing who they are and why they are fighting. The mirror moment is a revelation, a coming to Jesus, a watershed moment in the physical, emotional, and spiritual well-being of the hero.

James Scott Bell argues that if you start your story with this moment already in mind, it will help you write a better hero, which makes for a better story.

There's really no disadvantage to using this method. It's also one that you can easily pair with another method.

After all, if you're going to outline your novel, you should know your hero and what fuels him or her. Starting with the mirror moment can be extremely effective. Even if you don't use the mirror moment, chances are there will be a moment exactly like it somewhere in your novel.

SNOWFLAKE METHOD

·   ·   ·

The Snowflake method begins with a single sentence that sums up the essence of your book. It was created by Randy Ingermanson in his book *How to Write a Novel Using the Snowflake Method.*

Then, you expand that sentence into two sentences, then a paragraph. Before long, you have a working book description with your hook front and center. That description becomes the jumping off point for plotting your story, which evolves like a snowflake, branching out and forming a unique structure.

The advantage of the Snowflake Method is that you begin with marketing. How many times have you heard the expression "bake the marketing into your book?" That's exactly what this method helps you do. After all, you're writing your book's hook first and making it clear. If you can get that right, it will guide you throughout the entire novel writing process. This method is for people who need some structure, but also some room to play.

The disadvantage to the snowflake method is that it feels like one big brainstorming session. It also may not be appropriate for all genres. The method asks you to consider your marketing, and some people may not be able to wear a marketing hat and a writer hat at the same time. But it can be a highly effective method if you follow it.

LESTER DENT'S PLOT FORMULA

Lester Dent was a pulp fiction writer most famous for the Doc Savage series in the 1930s. He published a "formula" for writing mystery short stories, and that formula can just as easily be applied to novels with a bit of love and care.

For a 50,000-word novel with the Dent formula, you would divide it into four equal parts of 12,500 words.

- **Part 1**: Put the hero in trouble, introduce the cast as soon as possible, put the hero into an actual physical conflict, and end with a plot twist.
- **Part 2**: Put the hero in more trouble, make him or her struggle, introduce another physical conflict, and end with a plot twist.
- **Part 3:** Put the hero in even more trouble, allow him to make some progress against the villain, put the hero in another physical conflict, and end with a plot twist.
- **Part 4**: Put the hero in the worst possible trouble (almost to the point of death), make the hero escape with his own skills, clear up remaining mysteries, and defeat the villain. The short should of course end with a final twist.

I've simplified the formula for this book, but those are the core elements. Dent spends a lot of time talking about "trouble," what it means, and how to use conflict as a way to keep readers turning the page.

The advantage with this method is that it really is a formula. Lester Dent was one of the most successful pulp writers of his time, so if it worked for him, it could work for you.

The disadvantage of this method is that it's intended for mystery novels, and as I said before, you'll have to tweak it for other genres. If you spend some time understanding this method, though, it can help you write a fast-paced story full of action.

SCENES & SEQUELS

•   •   •

This is a method from Dwight V. Swain in his bestselling book, *Techniques of the Selling Writer*. Swain writes about a lot of storytelling methods, and his book is a bit dated, but the scenes and sequels method is by far the biggest takeaway from the book that still has modern appeal.

Scenes and sequels is an answer-call method that focuses on the momentum of your story. Swain argues that how you arrange your scenes is paramount to the reader experience.

In a scene, the hero is active. They're fighting bad guys or exploring a new area of town or finding clues to a mystery. The hero is moving the story forward through their actions.

In a sequel, which directly follows a scene (and honestly is just a scene by another name), the character is reactive. They're reacting to something that happened in the scene, and that reaction fosters character development.

I liken the scenes and sequels method to Isaac Newton's third law: for every action, there is an equal and opposite reaction.

Basically, with this method, you layer scenes and sequels on top of each other in order to keep readers reading.

The advantage of this method is that it has a loose enough structure to help you know what you should be doing, but enough slack to let you play around.

The disadvantage of this method is that it can feel quite tedious if you have a big novel.

STORY GRID

The Story Grid by Shawn Coyne is way too complicated to explore here. It is a painstaking approach that maps out every single point that should happen in the story, almost mathematically.

I don't use the Story Grid because I prefer flexibility, but it has been growing in popularity in the last few years because it appeals to those detail-oriented writers who like to have everything settled before writing.

Personally, I believe this method is too difficult and complex for most writers, especially beginners. I don't think anyone should spend this amount of time on outlining a novel, but I understand the appeal, and Shawn Coyne knows his stuff.

If you use this method, remember what I talked about earlier in this chapter about chapter-by-chapter outlining.

BEATS & PRE-PRODUCTION

This method was created by Sean Platt, Johnny B. Truant, and Dave Wright of Sterling & Stone.

Beats are a narrative version of your outline. Instead of using bullet points or rough notes, you write a few paragraphs about what happens in every chapter. The nice part about beats is that you're writing them in almost the same way that you'd write a novel, so it inspires some creative flow.

Pre-production follows the movie preproduction process. You scout locations for your settings and cast your characters, storing them in Evernote or Scrivener to refer to later as you're writing. Pinterest is a great tool for doing this.

The advantage of this method is that beats help you connect emotionally with the story and get excited about writing. The pre-production method is great to use whether you use beats or not.

The disadvantage of this method is that you may not want

to spend the time writing paragraphs of narrative when you could be writing your book itself.

When you combine beats and pre-production, you have a new and interesting flavor of outlining that can serve you well and help you think differently.

PANTSING: WRITING WITHOUT AN OUTLINE

What if you don't want to outline your novel?

Yes! You've come to the right place!

In fact, this might be one of the few nonfiction books for writers out there that has detailed advice for pantsers.

I haven't outlined a novel in a very long time, and this has been one of the secrets to my productivity, so if you're a pantser or think you might be, read on.

WHAT WE TALK ABOUT WHEN WE TALK ABOUT PANTSING

I could simply tell you to not outline a novel, but I suspect that won't be enough for you.

The common questions I usually hear are: How do I know what to write? What happens if I get stuck?

I won't lie and tell you that pantsing is easy.

The advantage of plotting is that you (kind of sort of) know what's going to happen in your story before you write it. Even if your story changes direction from your outline, you still have a structure to fall back on. That's powerful.

With pantsing, you're completely in the dark, but it has enormous benefits if you embrace it.

Not knowing what you're going to write forces you to trust your instinct.

You read books, right? Trust me when I say that all the books you read up to this point have definitely made an impact on you subconsciously. Writing without an outline helps you connect with your subconscious, and it creates a channel for those influences and techniques to flow through onto the page. When you outline, you simply aren't doing this because you're using the left side of your brain. Inspiration and flow come from the right side of your brain.

One of the most important lessons I teach in my books, my podcast, and my YouTube channel is that writers must learn to follow their instincts. School teachers, writing coaches, and even other writers teach the opposite. They teach you how to apply commonly-accepted writing best practices to your work so that you can reverse-engineer your fiction into something that readers want. Personally, I don't know that this approach works for most writers. I believe that the best way to learn how to write is to learn how to get out of your own way and trust your instinct, which means fighting fear and throwing common wisdom out the window if it doesn't suit your purposes.

PANTSING IS ABOUT CONQUERING YOUR FEAR

Let's talk about fear because it's real when you're writing without an outline.

Whether you outline your book or not, everything you want in your writing career lies on the other side of fear.

But the fear you face with outlining is different from the fear with pantsing.

With outlining, the fear is usually around second-guessing yourself.

With pantsing, the fear is more visceral. It will make you question if you should even be writing in the first place. If you can overcome this kind of fear, you can overcome anything.

Writing without an outline is also a way to guarantee that you'll have a long-term career. If you always know what you're going to write, you might eventually get bored. If writing is a discovery, however, then that can prevent burnout. I don't have any hard data to support this, but I suspect that many long-term writers no longer outline because they no longer need to.

If you want to learn more about writing without an outline, check out *Writing into the Dark* by Dean Wesley Smith, which in my opinion is the definitive book on this topic. It completely changed how I think about writing.

I've also devoted an entire book to conquering fear and writing without an outline, and it's called *Be a Writing Machine* (it's the next book in this series).

Fear manifests itself in many ways. There's fear of inadequacy, fear of failure, fear of success, fear of judgment by others, and so on.

The key to success with pantsing is that you have to learn to not give a shit. Don't give a shit about what people think, what people think you should do (outlining), what readers will think, whether you'll fail, etc. Merely thinking about any of that will derail you and stop you from finishing your novel.

Instead, you must be ruthless and learn to listen to your instinct. Whatever it tells you to do, do it, and do not contradict it unless you have a very good reason for doing so.

In *Writing into the Dark*, Dean Wesley Smith makes a very strong argument: your brain has a critical voice and a creative voice.

The critical voice is the left side of your brain; it operates through logic. The critical voice is also the "inner critic" that we talk so much about in the writing community. It will tell you that you're not good enough, that you can't do this.

The creative voice is the right side of your brain, and it operates through play. The creative voice has no limits and loves the freedom of expression.

However, the creative voice is a whisper and the critical voice is a yell. All it takes is you believing your critical voice to make your creative voice clam up and stop playing.

Put another way, outlining comes from the critical voice. You're using logic to piece together your story based on "rules" laid out by other writers.

Pantsing, however, is writing in its purest and most engaging form because when done right (and well), you're allowing your creative voice to play.

Another argument that Dean makes in his book (and in his courses) is that your creative voice knows everything there is to know about writing a story; the reason writers fail to write engaging stories isn't that they lack the skill—it's because they unintentionally suppress the creative voice.

When you read, watch movies, listen to music, etc., you subconsciously absorb writing techniques. The way that you "unlock" those techniques is through a focused, purposeful study of the craft and suppressing your critical voice so that your creative voice can create with no limitations. And then, you must learn to listen to your creative voice so that your stories shine.

Does that seem overwhelming? If it does, that's okay. But I have to warn you that the way many writers view "pantsing" is akin to "winging it." Very few pantsers advocate for a rigorous study of the craft. But I believe that if you want to succeed at pantsing, you have to be even more dedicated to the craft.

If you think pantsing is for you, here is what I want you to think about as you prepare to write your novel:

- Read regularly to stimulate your creative voice.
- Study the books that you enjoy on a regular basis, ignore the ones that you don't. When you study books, study them purposefully, analyzing the techniques that capture your imagination. Then learn how to replicate those techniques in your own work.
- Write your novel. As you write, do your best to ignore all fear and keep pushing through. While I don't believe in "writer's block" in the common sense of the word, I do believe that you need to learn how to combat your fears.
- Learn to "listen" for your creative voice. It's a whisper at first, but as you learn to suppress your fear, it will become louder, so much that you will know it whenever it speaks.
- Do not stray from what your creative voice recommends. Imagine that every book is your version of the Hero's Journey and you are the hero. The creative voice is the "mentor." Listen and let it guide you. When things get rough (particularly in the murky middle), remember its advice.

Don't let this chapter intimidate you. Pantsing does get easier the more you do it. I'll cover techniques to combat fear and writer's block later in this book. In the meantime, if you decide to go the pantsing route, embrace it, face your fears, and enjoy the ride.

EVEN IF YOU OUTLINE, YOU'RE STILL A PANTSER

Trust me: I am not knocking outlining. Even though it's no longer my preferred method, outlining helped me write a lot of good novels, so I could never say that it's not helpful. For this reason, I've learned to keep investing in understanding it because the principles behind some of the outlining methods do give you some great insights into the craft.

But even if you outline, there is going to come a day when you must pants.

Example #1: Short stories. Very few writers I know outline short stories. Writing short stories is a masterclass in learning how to pants, and it's why some people avoid them.

Example #2: Chapter-by-chapter outlining. It's a fact that you can't outline every single detail in your story. Sometimes you'll find yourself writing entire chapters that you didn't plan for. When you do that without the assistance of an outline, you are pantsing by definition. This can be a scary time if you're an outliner, but if you listen to your creative voice, you'll be just fine.

In fact, there are "pantsing" gaps in every novel that has an outline, so pantsing is still a skill you should learn to cultivate.

And pantsers—don't think I'm going to let you finish this chapter without telling you that outlining is a valuable skill for you to learn too.

Example #1: Collaborating with another author. It would be pretty hard to write a novel where two or more writers follow their creative voices entirely. Actually, it would be a train wreck. I don't know that I would do a collaboration on a novel without outlining.

Example #2: If you ever decide to submit your book to a traditional publisher, they may ask you for an outline. Better know how to do it if you want to pursue this path!

As I said at the beginning of this chapter, learning how to write a novel with and without an outline are both valuable skills.

WRITING YOUR NOVEL

It's time to rock!

We're going to pretend your book is outlined (or not), there's a steaming mug of coffee on your desk, and your music playlists are organized. Your writing app is open, and you just need to put your fingers on the keyboard and start typing.

You're ready to get started, but...you're in a staring match with the blinking cursor.

Don't underestimate the power of that cursor. I've seen it reduce grown men and women into blubbering babies.

In this chapter, I'm going to walk you through everything you need to win the battle with that blinking cursor.

But first, a rant.

DON'T WRITE SLOPPY FIRST DRAFTS!!!

. . .

You've probably heard the common advice:

- "Write shitty first drafts."
- "Don't worry about quality. Just get your book down
  on the page and fix it later."

Listen very carefully: I need you to take that advice and forget it. Right now. Please.

Crappy first drafts are the worst thing you can do, especially for your first novel. Nothing sucks the joy out of the novel writing process faster than bad first drafts.

Here's why:

- You write a shitty first draft. You feel an adrenaline
  rush at first. You've written a novel!
- After the adrenaline fades, you realize just how
  shitty your first draft is.
- That makes you feel like shit.
- Revision becomes a battle, with you rewriting
  scenes that you rushed through the first time. By the
  time you've finished your third or fourth draft, you
  are SICK of the novel. If you really struggle, you'll
  wonder if the next novel is worth it.
- The process begins all over again, but you begin
  with a little less enthusiasm at the beginning.

This, my friends, is what I call the emotional rollercoaster. Every writer is different and experiences a slightly different run of emotions, but the truth is that all of this can be avoided if you stop writing sloppy first drafts.

I don't know why writers insist on intentionally inflicting themselves with this kind of pain. It's the equivalent of self-flagellation.

Remember, learning how to be a writer is about learning how to eliminate fear.

A sloppy first draft reinforces fear because you'll second-guess yourself when you write the second draft. It's impossible not to if you just threw words onto the page.

A sloppy first draft also dramatically increases the amount of time you'll spend in revision.

Think about it like this. If you were a homebuilder and you built a "sloppy first draft" of a house, you'd piss off the homeowner and the city inspector, and they'd make you tear the home down and build it right. You'd spend double if not triple the time (and money) rebuilding it the right way. So why not just do it right the first time? Why not lay the foundation correctly, frame the house correctly, install the floors correctly, and put the roof on correctly? Why not do that, and then spend time revising little details if needed?

Writers don't think this way. Instead, they prefer to vomit onto the page and then try to make sense of it later, not realizing the emotional trouble it causes.

Now don't misunderstand me. I'm NOT telling you to be a perfectionist. I'll razz on perfectionism later, don't worry.

I'm also NOT telling you to write your entire novel in one draft (though that could be a goal for you down the road).

I'm simply telling you to treat your first draft with respect. You will be more confident when it's time to revise, and you will cut the time you spend revising, allowing you to publish faster so you can move on to your next book.

Have you ever heard the saying, "Treat your money well and it will treat you well?" The same principle applies to your writing. Treat your writing with respect and you'll be surprised at what your writing will do for you.

I know I'm a contrarian here, but I would much rather you

take a little longer to finish your novel than agonize through revision.

Now how exactly do you write better first drafts?

Read on.

Fɪʀsᴛ ɪᴍᴘʀᴇssɪᴏɴs ᴀʀᴇ ᴇᴠᴇʀʏᴛʜɪɴɢ, and your opening line is the first impression your book gives to readers.

A good opening line (and opening paragraph by extension) is more art than science, but for me personally, it should pass three tests:

- Does it make everything around the reader come to a screeching halt?
- Does it tease the novel without revealing too much?
- Is it funny, shocking, arresting, or weird?

If your opening line can pass those three prongs, you're off to a good start. Let's look at a few opening lines from best-selling novels and see how they do it.

"Cecilia Randall had heard of people who, if granted one wish, would choose to live their lives over again." - Debbie Macomber, *16 Lighthouse Road*

"My name is Odd Thomas, though in this age when fame is the altar at which most people worship, I am not sure why you should care who I am or that I exist." - Dean Koontz, *Odd Thomas*

"They found him in Ponta Porã, a pleasant little town in Brazil, on the border of Paraguay, in a land still known as the Frontier." - John Grisham, *The Partner*

"By the time she was eight, Mackenzie Elliot had been married fourteen times." - Nora Roberts, *Vision in White*

"*Umber whunnnn.*" - Stephen King, *Misery*

"A man with binoculars. That is how it began: with a man standing by the side of the road, on a crest overlooking a small Arizona town, on a winter night." - Michael Crichton, *The Andromeda Strain*

I won't analyze these lines because they speak for themselves. Each one has a different style and flavor. But they work because they are simple. Readers don't need very much; they just need to be intrigued.

OPENING LINE STEP-BY-STEP CHECKLIST

If you don't know what to write:

- Go to Amazon. Close your eyes and click around in the Kindle bestseller lists until you come to a random novel. Open a free sample and write down the opening line.
- Do this again for five or six more novels at random.
- Pick the line that resonated with you the most and made you want to keep reading. Spend a minute or two analyzing it and why it potentially worked.
- Write an opening line similar to the one that you picked. Don't plagiarize or infringe on anyone's copyright, but use it as inspiration and as a starting point for your own opening.

When you've written your opening line and paragraph, apply the three-prong test:

- Does everything around the reader come to a screeching halt? Can you imagine that happening?
- Does it tease the novel without revealing too much?
- Is it funny, shocking, arresting, or weird? Don't try too hard.

How to write this cleanly in your first draft:

- Don't try too hard, and don't be a perfectionist.
- Keep it simple.
- Keep the opening paragraph short. Just a couple of short to medium sentences is all you need. Let the opening paragraph stand on its own so you can maximize that first impression.
- Don't be trite. Avoid things like characters getting out of bed, being born, or doing trivial tasks. Readers read because they want to escape everyday life. Nothing bores them faster than a character waking up.

What to do in revision:

- It's okay to spend some time tweaking your opening line and paragraph to give them the best impact, but don't go overboard.
- Consider sharing (just) your opening paragraph or page with beta readers to get their opinion on whether it passes the three-prong test. It's better if those beta readers are people who read books regularly in your genre because they can tell you how the book compares to other similar books.

FIRST 500 WORDS

Your opening line and paragraph should hook the reader. The first 500 words keep them reading.

Many writers are tempted to jump into the action, but that can be a mistake.

If you read the works of the mega-bestsellers, they do the opposite. For them, the first 500 words are about establishing the character, the setting, and the conflict. Only then do they catapult the reader into the story.

If you look at virtually any novel by James Patterson, John Grisham, Nora Roberts, etc.—they all do this, and it happens like clockwork: first 500 words, and then the story.

Think of the first 500 words of your story like a racehorse in the few seconds before the gates open. The horse is anxious—every muscle in its body is tense as a spring, ready to explode. Yet there is a certain amount of zen in those seconds too.

The best way to introduce a character is to put the reader in his or her head while they deal with a problem. That problem doesn't have to be huge. It just has to give some insight into who the character is, and start them on the path to the bigger conflict.

How do you do that?

Show...don't tell...

I cringed when I wrote that sentence because so many people just say it but then don't elaborate.

What does "show, don't tell" actually mean?

"Showing" means helping the reader experience every scene in five dimensions: sight, sound, taste, touch, and smell.

You do this through:

- Describing the setting through the eyes of the character, using only words and phrases that the character themselves would use. In other words, if your character wouldn't use "herbaceous" to describe a fragrance, you shouldn't use it to describe what they're smelling in your narrative.
- Using interesting and fresh descriptions to engage the reader's imagination. There are unlimited ways to do this, and good writers learn how to do this well and in a style of their own. When readers refer to a writer's "style," they are most often referring to the way the writer weaves sensory detail.

The five senses are the most effective way to hook readers. They suck the reader in and keep them "seeing" the story through the eyes of your character. As a writer, you should always be learning to find ways to sharpen your sensory details.

Think about the first 500 words like character manners—the reader has to be emotionally invested in the character before they'll commit to following them on their journey. If you met someone in real life, you wouldn't be friends with them immediately, right? You have to get to know them first. Nothing builds rapport between two people like experiencing a challenge together and overcoming it. Take the same approach with your character. It makes them more endearing.

When I learned how to do this (intentionally), my writing changed overnight.

A NOTE ABOUT WRITING THE FIVE SENSES

My general rule is to include the five senses in an opening wherever possible. I first learned this from Dean Wesley Smith, but then saw it used constantly by the mega-bestsellers, and they taught me how to do this on a deeper level.

What does using the five senses mean? After all, it's common fiction writing advice.

I won't give you a list of what you should include, because that would be a disservice to you.

Be creative.

But here are some considerations for each sense that I want you to think about:

- **Sight** is the easiest sense to write about, and the one you've probably already mastered. I challenge you to rethink your approach if this is the primary sense you're using.
- **Sound** is the second easiest sense to write about because you have a lot of options. You can describe a sound happening in the setting, the sound of a character doing something, or use an onomatopoeia. Even dialogue can be used as sound if someone is shouting or their voice trails off. Silence can be used as sound too. See what I mean about having choices?

- **Touch** is the sense with great opportunity for creativity but isn't always the first writers think of. After all, a character can only touch something so much, right? What about textures on surfaces that the character doesn't touch? For example, if you write that a spaceship has a lacquered exterior, that's a texture, and in my mind counts as touch, even though the character isn't physically touching it. Think broader about textures and how you can find opportunities to include them. Often, a simple adjective can make an important difference in the readers' sensory experience.

- **Smell** is another good sense that isn't always available. But look for ways to use it when you can, as it can be visceral when used, especially if there's an emotion tied to it.

- **Taste** is the least used of the senses in fiction. There's a time and a place for it. Most people think food, but there are other ways to insert taste. For example, in an example later in the chapter, I describe a character as having a salt and pepper beard. It's somewhat of a cliché, but you could argue that it qualifies. I would caution you about adding taste just to add it, but if there's an opportunity to describe this sense in your scene, use it as vividly as possible, as you don't always get the chance.

What if you can't use all the senses in a story? That's fine. Double up on another sense.

For example, if you can't write taste, double up on sound. If you can't write smell, double up on sight. Doing this deepens the reading experience and helps the reader go deeper even if all the senses may not be present.

When you do have the opportunity to incorporate the lesser used senses, jump on it and have some fun.

FIRST 500 WORDS STEP-BY-STEP CHECKLIST

If you don't know what to write:

1. When in doubt, describe the setting in the five senses through the eyes of the character. Don't do it all at once; pick one or two senses and focus on making them feel real.
2. Imagine what your main character is feeling at that very moment in the story. Are they pissed? Scared? Happy? In a couple of sentences, show the reader those feelings.
3. Back to the setting. Can you use more sensory details?
4. Describe how the character got into that situation.
5. Segue into the story, with the character dealing with the conflict.
6. If you do this right, you should be pretty close to 500 words when you include your opening paragraph. If you're a little short or long, don't worry about it. Start the story!

Next level:

- The above checklist is formulaic, but it's not, actually. Remember story DNA!

How to write this cleanly in your first draft:

- Is there a clear setting?
- Is there a clear conflict that threatens the character?
- Are your sensory descriptions on-point and free of clichés?
- If the reader were describing your novel to a friend, would they be able to clearly state what your character's problem is, and how they got there?
- Avoid overly long openings. Many writers feel the need to write long, long paragraphs to set up the story, usually all narrative with all fluff. You don't need to do that.

What to do in revision:

- If you follow the steps above, the only work you should need to do is revisit the individual elements to make sure that they are as effective as they can be. Resist the urge to do major rewrites.

AN EXAMPLE

. . .

Here is an example of the first 500 words from my book *Death Marked*, co-written with my friend Justin Sloan.

I share examples from my work not to brag, but to show you that I practice what I preach.

This one doesn't quite have all five senses, because it wasn't appropriate for the scene. To compensate, I doubled up on sight and feel so that the reader could feel the intense cold in the scene.

See if you can spot the items from the checklist and pay attention to how they're woven in. I use all of the techniques in this book every day when I show up to the page.

When Rohan's fiancée died, he'd had no idea it would lead him to the snow-covered slopes of the Ural Mountains, searching for a way to speak with her one last time.

Closure, he told himself as he trudged through the snow—that's all he wanted. Unless, as he'd hoped, there was a slight chance he could bring her back.

A gust of wind sent snow swirling around him, its chill reaching through his layers of long underwear, sweater, and parka. Ice crystals clung to his cheeks like small needles, biting him with their cold every time the wind blew. Yet, somehow, sweat slicked his back. None of it was anything compared to the burning in his chest, however, at the thought of seeing Senna again. To hear her voice, press his lips against hers.... There wasn't anything that could dampen his excitement, not even this cold.

Howling gusts of wind brought a flurry of snow before Rohan. He tucked his head into the folds of his parka and focused on pushing forward, one step at a time. Suddenly, the wind changed direction and the wall collapsed, revealing craggy slopes that slanted upward into the white sky. Rohan stumbled as the ground shook.

Footsteps crunched behind him in warning before a hand gripped his shoulder. Altemus. Rohan nodded, wondering if he looked as haggard as this old man, his gray whiskers held together in clumps of ice. Heavy purple bags sagged from his eyes, barely visible under the skullcap that he wore beneath his parka hood. He still hadn't explained the rifle slung over his shoulder.

"We're almost there," Altemus said, his voice thick with confidence.

"I hope you're right," Rohan said, rubbing his hands. They'd gone numb, and he couldn't feel them through his gloves.

"We can stop if you like," Altemus said, but his eyes had already moved to the gray mountain slopes, almost invisible in the darkness.

Every part of Rohan's body begged him to say yes, but he resented the suggestion. Altemus did this kind of psychiatrist crap all the time—he'd say one thing when he meant the opposite. It might have worked on his patients, but Rohan wasn't going to let the old man manipulate him. Clearly, the old man didn't understand the extremes that Rohan was willing to go, the months spent in bed, staring at pictures of him and Senna, once happy. When she had left him, it was like she'd torn out part of his soul—he could never be whole without her. So he wouldn't rest until they were together again.

Rohan shook his head and said, "Nothing can stop me now."

THE REST OF YOUR FIRST CHAPTER

You've hooked readers with your opening paragraph. You've kept them reading through your first 500 words.

Now it's time for the story to begin.

Your character should be dealing with a conflict of some kind.

Remember the story DNA? It will come in handy here.

Use dialogue to flavor the first chapter (if you have dialogue in the first chapter; you may not).

Use narrative and continue to use the five senses to help the reader see the story.

Use action to drive the story forward.

Think of it as a boxing match. A boxer moves around his opponent with good footwork. He jabs. Ducks. Sidesteps. Hooks. Misses a punch. Misses another punch. Jabs. He uses the same portfolio of moves, but he adjusts in the moment depending on what's happening. That's why boxing is so interesting to watch. If a boxer did nothing but throw right hooks, he'd probably get knocked out.

As you write the rest of your first chapter, focus on telling the story through DNA by having the character deal with the conflict.

REMAINING CHAPTER 1 CHECKLIST

If you don't know what to write:

- Remember story DNA. If you've made it this far, you already know exactly how to develop a chapter.

Next level:

- End the chapter on a cliffhanger. Just as the hero is about to finish the conflict, introduce a plot twist or simply find a way to end the chapter and then pick up in Chapter 2. Some people may disagree with me about cliffhangers in general, but one thing we can all agree on is that your first chapter is critical. Start late, end early. It will keep readers turning the page. Your sole focus with Chapter 1 is to get readers to read Chapter 2.
- In total, a good first chapter has a great opening line and paragraph, establishes the hero, shows them dealing with a conflict, and that ends on a cliffhanger so that readers will read the next chapter.

How to write this cleanly in your first draft:

- You already know how to do it. Once you've mastered the art of the opening chapter, every chapter in your book that follows is just a variation on this method.

What to do in revision:

- Nothing, if you do your job correctly the first time!

CHAPTER OPENINGS

Your chapter openings are important because they re-engage the reader with the story.

A chapter is a refresh. Like a scene change in a movie, a chapter performs a pattern interrupt in the reader's brain, which keeps them interested. Most fiction books have short to medium chapters for this reason.

I've already taught you how to open your book; if you can do that, you can write chapter openings.

I've been reading and studying the works of mega-best-selling authors (Grisham, Patterson, Rowling, etc.) for years. Even though each author is wildly different, they follow similar techniques if you pay close attention.

I noticed that they use only three types of chapter openings. There are variations, to be sure, but you can look at any chapter opening of a mega-bestseller and slot it into one of three categories.

This section includes explanations of those categories, followed by examples of each.

. . .

THE STANDARD OPENING

The standard opening is a bread and butter approach. In this type of opening, you set up the scene by describing the setting with sensory details, putting the reader inside the character's head, and making sure this is established before advancing into the plot.

Put more simply, it includes:

- A clear setting
- Sensory details in all five senses
- Description of what the character is feeling, how they got there, and why
- "Clean break" or turn of thought that segues into the story

When done right, you can tell when the opening transitions into the story. The turn of thought is usually clear. Personally, I think this is very pleasant because it serves as a mini pattern interrupt. I see this all the time in books now. As a reader, I never noticed them because, when done right, they're invisible.

This opening type is simple and clean, and it never fails if you do it right.

THE ABSTRACT OPENING

I've also heard this referred to a "summary opening" by Dean Wesley Smith.

In this opening type, the chapter usually begins with narrative. It could be backstory, historical context, or a recounting of events that led up to the current situation. It's usually told by the narrator, and while there may be sensory details, the focus is on conveying a story or abstraction to the reader.

A good example of this is *Jurassic Park* by Michael Crichton. The first chapter is a recount of (seemingly) real events in the bioengineering field that led up to the events in Isla Nublar.

The goal of the abstract opening is to root the reader in the "lore" of the world so that when the main character comes onto the scene, the readers like him or her even more. It also gives context to the setting.

Whereas the standard opening begins with clarity—a clear setting, a clear main character, a clear conflict, clear sensory details, and so on—the abstract opening begins with abstraction. Instead of a character in a setting, you begin with a concept, and that concept slowly progresses into clarity. In some respects, you're "telling" and not "showing," and it's one of the few times when this is okay.

It's like being at the eye doctor and having lenses switched in front of your eyes—everything's blurry at first, but after a few rounds, you can see clearly.

Put another way, an abstract opening is like a movie scene when the camera focus is fuzzy—there's lots of bokeh and blurred shapes—and then the camera focus sharpens, showing you the setting in a stylized way.

This opening method depends entirely on your POV. If it's in the first person, then you still have to obey the rules of staying inside their head. In the third person, there's more of an art to it.

The first key with an abstract opening—and most beginning writers miss it—is to keep it within 500 words wherever possible. Just because you're exploring a concept doesn't mean that you have a license to go on forever.

The second key with an abstract opening is to use sensory details whenever you can, since this opening type is almost always written in a "telling" way. You don't get a pass on writing clearly with this type of opening. Even if you're explaining, say, a historical event, help readers see it. Imagine it like a documentary—how can you help the reader feel like they're there, especially since you're "telling?"

The elements of an abstract opening:

- An opening statement that sets the tone.
- History/lore/mythology/concept/recounting of a specific event (your options are unlimited).
- "Clean break" or turn of thought that transitions into the story. In some cases, this is best done as a section break, but every story and chapter have different demands.
- Once you've moved into clarity, proceed with a standard opening. Yes, you have to do double the work, but if you do it right, readers will be steeped in your story and they won't want to leave.

You should use abstract openings sparingly. It's easy for a beginner to get them wrong, but I believe in experimenting and trying things, especially if it's your first novel.

Just remember to keep within the 500-word mark as a general practice. Remember, readers don't want to read pages and pages of exposition that has no purpose.

This is a good tool to have in your toolbox. I've found it to be extremely effective after there is a major passing of time in the story. It can be useful in other situations too—the only limit is your imagination. The best way to learn how to do abstract openings is to start looking for them when you're reading novels you enjoy.

. . .

THE COLD OPENING

I named this after the common film term where the movie just starts right in the middle of the action without any establishment of the character or the setting.

If done in the first chapter, it can sometimes be disorienting to the reader, and it might take them a minute to figure out what's going on. For your purposes, I recommend that you not open your first novel's opening chapter with a cold opening.

If done in later chapters, it's a way for the writer to bypass details to keep the reader reading. For example, if the hero visits ancient ruins and has spent the last chapter or two in the same room in the ruins, you may not need to keep re-establishing the setting because it would be redundant.

The most common way to do a cold opening is to start a chapter with dialogue. It puts the reader right in the middle of the action. As with anything in writing, the only limit is your imagination.

Doing a cold opening doesn't relieve you of your obligation to write with sensory details. You still need them. The cold opening simply begins with the plot instead of lead-up to the plot.

A cold opening should not be an excuse for lazy writing. It's a pacing tool to keep your readers engaged. After all, if you did a standard opening or a summary opening every time, that might be too much, and it would bore your readers. The cold opening helps you add variety.

COMBINING OPENING TYPES

. . .

When you chain these three opening types together, you end up with a rhythm.

My rule of thumb is to use a standard opening any time the setting changes. It keeps the reader established in the world.

If the setting doesn't change, then I use my best judgment—does the scene take place in a different area of the setting? If so, then I will do a standard opening. If not, then I may do a cold opening or find a common ground between the two.

When you think about opening types as a rhythm, you have a pretty powerful tool. Your novel openings might look something like this:

- Chapter 1: Hero is chased through a jungle by soldiers. (Standard opening)
- Chapter 2: Hero evades soldiers and retreats into an abandoned spaceship near a river. (Standard opening)
- Chapter 3: Hero tends to a flesh wound inside the safety of the ship, tries to figure out what to do next. (Standard opening)
- Chapter 4: Soldiers attack hero in the spaceship. Battle ensues but the hero is captured. (Cold opening)
- Chapter 5: Flashback of hero's past. Hero wakes up in jail. (Summary opening, standard opening).

This is a simple example, but hopefully, you can see how the openings work in tandem with the content of the story.

Don't discount the power of your chapter openings. They're incredibly effective!

SOME EXAMPLES

. . .

Here are a group of openings. This is a different book, but all the examples below are from the first half of it.

They are from my book *Honor's Reserve*, Book 1 in my Galaxy Mavericks space opera series. The story follows Grayson McCoy, a member of the Galactic Guard whose life changes forever when he uncovers a sinister scheme by two criminals who aren't what they seem when he stops their spaceship due to suspicious activity.

Don't worry so much about the story because there are gaps between the chapters, and these are just excerpts. Just read it and analyze the elements. Pay attention to how they work and draw your own conclusions about how you could do this in your own work or change the approach for your novel.

STANDARD OPENING EXAMPLE

From the bridge of the Galactic Guard Cutter Horizon, Petty Officer Grayson McCoy shone a spotlight into dark space, onto a lone starship slowing as it cut its engine. Two white, blinking lights appeared on the roof. A yellow gravity ring rotated clockwise around the center of the ship.

"I've got a visual," Grayson said, locking the ship in his sights. "Engine's off."

He kept his eyes on the ship and swept the light up and down the hull. It was a sleek passenger ship, leisure grade, big enough for fourteen people. Most private passenger ships usually had salons, living quarters, kitchens, and bathrooms. This one looked like it had all of that, plus a hyperdrive. Its long white wings gave it the look of a dove floating among the stars.

He scanned the side of the ship where the name and port of call should have been.

There was nothing—the side of the ship was blank.

He glanced over at a black-haired, tanned man in a headset and an olive green flight suit who was bent over an instrument panel.

"What do you think?" Grayson asked.

Petty Officer Romeo Beauregard radioed to the base. "We've located an unidentified starship near the nebula border. No name or port of call."

Beauregard waited for a response. A voice crackled in his headset. "Base says to proceed with boarding."

It wasn't every day that Grayson came across a ship like this. Most of the time, boarding a regular private passenger vessel was boring. But boarding one with no name or I.D.—you never knew what to expect. He preferred search and rescues, but this might be interesting.

He stopped the spotlight on the ship's bridge, a large glass bubble on the front of the ship. A man and a woman put their hands over their faces.

"We've got a male, late thirties, maybe six-two, salt and pepper beard. A woman that looks like his wife, late twenties, black hair."

He heard a computerized chime behind him. The rotunda-shaped bridge of the Galactic Guard ship was quiet.

Petty Officer Will Stroud, the flight mechanic, was sitting at his instrument panel, its green lights illuminating his face and red hair. "I charted their path. They're not from our galaxy, guys."

Outsiders. Or travelers returning home. In any case, they were still subject to the laws of the Rah Galaxy, and to searches from the Guard.

Beauregard swiveled in his chair and motioned to Grayson.

He wore his trademark calm expression, the look of wisdom and experience. He was probably only a few years older than Grayson. He was an active duty petty officer, first class. As the only original active duty Guard on board, he took it as his responsibility to train Grayson and Will. He used everything as a learning experience.

"Grayson, what do you think?" Beau asked.

Grayson glanced back out at the ship. Things were quiet in space. "Looks fairly innocuous to me, but you never know."

"Let's see if you're right."

ABSTRACT OPENING EXAMPLE

Sometime, around a thousand years ago, a scientist on Earth had the bright idea of sending human and animal DNA into space. Since aliens were more intelligent than us, he reasoned, and since humans had yet to meet them, this would be a peace offering. He believed that they might be able to unlock the secrets of our DNA and visit Earth with knowledge to bestow upon the human race.

This was, of course, during the famines and rapid warming of the planet.

He packed in DNA of all the major human races and ethnicities, but in a last-minute gamble, he included animal DNA too. Horses. Cows. Lions. Spiders.

And pigs.

He sent the package into space onboard a nanocraft that could travel at twice the speed of light.

The scientist was universally mocked and he died having achieved nothing.

No one heard from the spacecraft for nine hundred and

fifty years, until a race of anthropomorphic pigs was spotted on an Earthlike planet in the Argus Galaxy.

Scientist scratched their heads at how an alien race could be as intelligent as pigs, look like pigs, and walk on two feet. A full-blown scan of their DNA found remnants of the very samples that had been sent into space so long ago.

Scientists think that the nanocraft collided with an asteroid that had some kind of molecular life on it, and that that asteroid crashed onto an Earthlike planet that supported carbon life. The two life forms mixed, rapidly evolved, and Arguses were born—a barbaric, scavenger race that served as a reminder of home in all the wrong ways.

At least that's how they taught it to Grayson in the history books.

COLD OPENING EXAMPLE

"What do you see?" Beauregard asked.

Grayson shut off the oxygen in his suit to conserve it. Then he unlocked the hatch on the airlock wall, revealing the hostages again. Looking at them closer, he noticed that they were crammed into a small hallway, packed so tightly they couldn't move.

"Looks like at least a dozen people," Grayson said, studying the victims. They looked at him with frightened eyes. "They all have burns across their bodies. No clothes. This must be a short trip since they're packed in there naked."

"Can you talk to them?"

"Negative. They're gagged."

He felt his way across the cold glass for a way to help the people out.

But there were no openings.

"They're sealed away by acrylic glass, approximately two inches thick," he said. "It's strong enough to withstand the pressurizing and depressurizing of the airlock."

"Who'd've thought smugglers would be using airlocks to transport people?" Beauregard asked. "It's a big gamble."

"The gamble's paying off," Grayson said, feeling the glass some more. "I can't find an opening. My guess is that the criminals had these people crawl into here from somewhere else in the ship."

He placed his hand on the glass, next to the face of a naked woman, who was crying. Her tears streamed down and landed on the leg of a man, who rapped on the glass at Grayson. "They look pretty scared, Beau."

Grayson could hear Beauregard's consternation from the other side of the radio.

"I don't like it. You shouldn't be there. You should've let go."

"I'm here now," Grayson said. "And I'm going to see this through. Man, those two really scammed us. Near the end, I was almost starting to like them."

"I knew something was off. I just didn't know what."

Silence.

"How's Will?" Grayson asked.

"I got him," Beauregard said. "We're following you at full speed. They're moving pretty fast and it's hard to keep up. I think they're going to jump into hyperspace soon."

"Did you call reinforcements?"

"They're on the way. Grayson—"

"What?"

"I know you're not going to listen to me. But you're in a captive situation. If you want any good to come out of this, don't confront Rina and Gen. As far as they know, you're here with me on the ship, or worse, floating in space. It'll be more useful to—"

Beauregard's voice cut out.

"Beau?" Grayson asked. "I can't hear you."

The ship's computer beeped.

Entering hyperspace...

CHAPTER ENDINGS

Your chapter endings are important, but they're easy to ignore.

Chapter endings are prime real estate to exercise your craft expertise.

A good chapter opening keeps the reader engaged. A good chapter ending makes the reader NEED to turn the page.

You have more options with chapter endings because there are many different ways to end a scene.

Cliffhangers endings at the book level have a negative connotation, but they're absolutely essential at the chapter level, and they're one of the telltale differences between a skilled writer and an amateur.

With short to medium-sized chapters, it's hard to argue with how effective they are when you actually analyze the works of bestsellers. Almost every bestseller I have ever read writes irresistible chapter endings.

Fortunately, this is easy to do once you see it and learn what a good chapter ending looks like.

I'll cover some of the chapter ending types that I have seen used by bestsellers and that have worked well for me. This is not an exhaustive list, and understand that you can be as creative as you want, and you should absolutely experiment.

DECLARATORY ENDING

A declaratory ending ends with a declaratory sentence that introduces tension that makes the reader want to turn the page.

Here are some examples.

"She was screaming."

"A man in a balaclava stood in the bedroom, and he brandished a knife."

"The witness was dead."

"I was too late."

Often, this kind of ending is done simply, and it's good for doing reveals. The key is to introduce tension—the last image should be a shock.

.   .   .

MEDIA INSERT ENDING

In this type of ending, the character discovers some sort of media that creates a plot twist or introduces tension.

Maybe it's a photograph that reveals that someone the hero thought they trusted is actually friends with the villain.

Maybe it's a newspaper headline. Or a dictionary definition. Or a quote. Or the hero turning on the television and seeing the city being destroyed by a giant alien. You have lots of choices, and your story should naturally lead you to this type of ending. Don't force it. Learning that it exists is the first step in using it correctly.

The key is that whatever the medium is, it should shock the reader.

This is a fun way to end a chapter too, but you can go overboard.

PICTURESQUE ENDING

Imagine your chapter ending like a photograph. What would it look like?

This type of ending gives the reader a quick snapshot just before the narrative jumps ahead to the next chapter.

Here are some examples.

"The road wound upward through the snow, toward the craggy summit."

"Elliott raised the camera to his face, and the last thing I remember before the police took me away in handcuffs was the camera flashing, and him saying "Smile!""

"In the dense fog, it was only after the helicopter landed that we could see the immense waterfall before us—and the blue condo sitting atop the water, shining like a crown."

Imagine the reader seeing your story flow past in their mind's eye. Then, once your scene ends, pretend there's a camera shutter sound. Does that final line in the chapter make for a good photograph? If so, then you've got a picturesque ending.

DIALOGUE ENDING

Dialogue is a great way to end a chapter. Let a character reveal something or say something dramatic.

When done well, it adds drama and teases the next chapter. It also works best when there is foreshadowing.

Dialogue endings are the equivalent of giving your reader a single potato chip. They can't eat just one, so they'll turn the page for more!

For me personally, a good dialogue ending makes the reader:

- smile a little smile before turning the page, or

- utter a curse word before turning the page (because they're worried about the character, of course) or
- turn the page so quickly they almost rip it (or smudge the screen of their phone or e-reader)

Dialogue endings hook me as a reader. I fall for them every single time.

They're simple to do and have a big impact when you do them right. You can overdo them, though, so don't make all of your chapter endings finish with dialogue.

RESOLUTION ENDING

In this ending, your character resolves to do something.

Here are some examples:

"I knew what I had to do."

"I had to save my cousins. But first, I had to kick some ass."

The key with this ending type is to get the reader pumped for what's next or to keep them on the edge of their seat about how the character is going to accomplish what they resolve to do.

. . .

COMBINING ENDINGS WITH OPENINGS

Let's look at the example from the last chapter and add in endings so you can see how effective openings and endings can work together.

- Chapter 1: Hero is chased through a jungle by soldiers. Fight scene. Hero narrowly escapes but looks down and sees a wound on arm. (Standard opening, declaratory ending)
- Chapter 2: Hero loses the soldiers and discovers an abandoned spaceship near a river. (Standard opening, picturesque ending)
- Chapter 3: Hero medicates arm wound inside the safety of the ship, tries to figure out what to do next. Hero hears soldiers approaching, resolves to kill them if necessary. (Standard opening, resolution ending)
- Chapter 4: Soldiers attack hero in the spaceship. Battle ensues, but the hero is captured. (Cold opening, dialogue ending. "You're coming with us, asshole!")
- Chapter 5: Flashback of hero's past. Hero wakes up in jail and meets the villain, who ends the chapter by brandishing torture weapons, saying, "Nice to finally meet you, Hero. Now why don't we talk about why you were snooping around my facility in the jungle?" (Summary opening, standard opening, hybrid between a picturesque and dialogue ending)

Your endings are equally as important as your openings. Don't neglect them. Use cliffhangers and suspenseful endings whenever possible. You'll find that readers will hate you for doing it, in a good way.

SOME EXAMPLES

Here are some chapter endings from the same book, *Honor's Reserve*.

Again, just focus on the elements at work and don't pay attention too much to the story.

DECLARATORY ENDING EXAMPLE

Then he realized the purpose of the ship, a discovery that chilled him and sent him back to the darkest memories of his African ancestors.

Gen and Rina weren't smugglers.

They were slave traders.

MEDIA INSERT ENDING EXAMPLE

As they locked the coffin's wheels in place, Grayson glanced up at an easel that had his father's picture on it.

There he was, dapper in his favorite baby blue, button-down Oxford, posing in front of a white background, with those thick bifocals that Ma always hated. And that crescent moon smile— not quite smiling, but not frowning either.

A fitting picture.

He grabbed a program from a table.

Carter James McCoy
Hathaway Place

Carter McCoy, age 66, left the love of his life, Rose, on December 8, 3045. He was born December 18, 2979, in Hydrangea Heights to Arnold and Viola (Patton) McCoy.

Carter worked for over forty years for the Provenance Public Schools and retired as a Curriculum Specialist and Swim Coach.

He is survived by his wife, Rose, and his son, Grayson; his brother Ray and his family.

He was preceded in death by his brother, Miles; and his parents.

Memorials contributions may be directed to the Provenance Coast Guard Reserve in his loving memory.

When Grayson finished reading, he broke down.

PICTURESQUE ENDING EXAMPLE

Grayson followed Beauregard and the hostages onto the Galactic Cutter's air box, a small gray chamber that connected to the ship proper.

"It doesn't make any sense," Grayson said.

Beau pointed out the window. "We were just waiting for the right time to strike. And we had a little help."

Outside, through a small square window, Grayson saw the two Argus ships smoldering.

All around them, the gray frigates of the Galactic Naval Fleet shone in deep space.

DIALOGUE ENDING EXAMPLE

Grayson and Will looked at each other.

Then they drew their handcoils.

But Gen was at the airlock controls. He smacked the engage button and the lights in the airlock flashed red.

The pressure doors closed in front of Gen and Rina before Grayson and Will could fire.

"Crap!" Will cried.

A computer chimed.

Airlock opening in three, two...

"Grab on to something," Grayson said.

RESOLUTION ENDING EXAMPLE

Grayson turned to the wall of victims. "I'm going to get you out of here," he said. "But be patient for now, all right?"

And then he shut the hatch quietly over their faces, the fearful looks in their eyes burned into his memory forever.

"Beau?" he whispered.

But the communications were severed. The radio didn't work in hyperspace.

He was on his own now.

CHARACTER DEVELOPMENT

What about character development?

How do you develop your hero so that readers identify with him or her?

What about character arcs, emotional arcs, round characters, flat characters, foils, and all the other things they taught you in school?

Throw them out the window.

Yes, I'm telling you to throw out character arcs along with all the other stuff.

Why?

At this moment, someone somewhere is probably cursing my name and poking a voodoo doll with my face on it.

Let me explain.

The standard way writers are taught character development is to create a character arc. There are many different character arc methods out there, but the one thing they have in common is that they require you to develop your arc before you start writing. There are various "character sheets" you can fill out to help you with this.

This method often recommends that your character should

have this, you should make the reader feel that, have your character progress to the point of X by the 75% mark...

I believe that this advice is irrelevant and impractical BEFORE you start writing.

Here's why. Think back to the example I gave of character manners.

If I were to attend a cocktail party, would it be appropriate for me to make a list of people that would be attending, then decide before I even met them how I wanted to make them feel about me? Would it be appropriate to try to engineer their response?

I don't know about you, but that would be pretty disingenuous and downright manipulative.

If you wouldn't do this in real life, why would you do it with a character?

I know, I know—I'm drawing comparisons between fiction and reality, but readers don't see the line between the two. By the very nature of writing fiction, you're asking them to suspend their disbelief.

Your hero might as well be a real person to readers. Look at the reviews of any bestselling book and you'll see that readers identify with the characters, not the plot. They laugh and cry with your characters.

So...if you treat your characters like mere characters and not larger than life figures that readers expect them to be, then you're probably going to swing and miss.

And if you try to engineer a character that pushes readers' buttons at just the right times...well, I argue that it's going to come across flat.

Just as you wouldn't pre-engineer people's emotions in real life, you shouldn't do it with your characters. That's why I believe that mapping out character arcs before writing adds no value to the writing process.

Here's the secret I learned the hard way: character development happens on the page, in real-time, as you write.

This applies to virtually any character you write, not just the hero. You can and should develop supporting and minor characters too—just not as thoroughly.

I challenge you to think about character development differently.

I challenge you to change your understanding, broaden your perspective, and narrow your focus.

CHANGE YOUR UNDERSTANDING

Character development is not:

- Deciding how readers should feel. Only they decide that.
- Deciding how your character should feel. Only they decide that.
- Detailed emotional and psychological arcs prior to writing.

BROADEN YOUR PERSPECTIVE

Most writers I know think of character arcs as a series of events. The character does this, does that...

I need you to broaden your perspective.

Character development is:

- The character interacting with settings and other characters, and how the character responds to those interactions.
- The reader experiencing those settings and other characters, and forming their opinions about the story.
- The area between the hero's response and the reader's opinion.

In my day job, I am a manager. One of the hardest parts of my job is determining when to promote people and who to promote.

Here's the problem: you can have two equal people that do the same things, but the person that gets promoted is often the one who uses those experiences to develop themselves.

In other words, just because someone does something like attend a conference or obtain a mentor doesn't mean that they will be promoted. Anyone can check items off a list. How they respond to new events and experiences is how they develop, not the mere fact that they did them. What ultimately matters is how they use those experiences as a starting point to think differently and improve their work product, professionalism, or contacts—and how well they can articulate how the experience was genuinely meaningful to them.

So I challenge you to broaden your perspective. Instead of having a character simply do things, can you instead think about what those "things" do to the character? How does the character respond and feel? That's the essence of how people in real life grow and develop.

NARROW YOUR FOCUS

. . .

Character development is:

- The reader experiencing the struggles right alongside the character in real-time, through solid sensory details.
- Dialogue (internal and external) of the character.
- Narrative told through the perspective of the character.
- Actions of the character on the page.

In other words, character development is DNA...

You can map this stuff out all day long, but what ultimately matters is how you execute on the page.

And sorry, I don't care how adept an outliner you are. You can't outline DNA.

So what that you planned to have the character caress a puppy in the sixteenth chapter? Do you execute on it from a DNA perspective? Does the reader respect the character as a result of what you've written?

We all plan novels with the best of intentions.

But remember that outlines change...

Throughout the course of a story, characters change, even if you make plans...

Instead, listen to the character. Find ways to develop them on the page through DNA. Don't refer to fancy character arcs, because readers don't gauge a story based on its arc. When was the last time you heard a reader say, "I love this story because every point on the hero's character arc was painstakingly mapped out?" Not very often.

Instead, you hear stories of how the character felt real or felt like someone the reader knew. That kind of emotional impact doesn't happen through planning out an arc.

It happens through writing, listening to your instinct, and

focusing on what's on the page. It's the "micro-moments" that readers remember.

For example, I love Alex Cross novels by James Patterson.

In *Along Came a Spider*, there is a fantastic sequence of scenes where Alex Cross visits Miami to pay a ransom to a serial killer. In just a couple of chapters, you learn an incredible amount of information about Alex:

- While going for a quick swim at the hotel, he muses through narrative about how he always exercises anywhere he goes.
- He connects with the book's love interest, Jezzie Flanagan, who happens to be swimming at the same time as him. Over a few scenes, they have a sexual encounter, but not before Alex muses about the societal views on a black man sleeping with a white woman.
- The next day, Alex visits Disney World to pay the ransom. The payoff goes wrong, and he is taken hostage on a small plane traveling God-knows-where, with a mysterious man who takes the money and runs, leaving Alex to think quickly about how to escape. Except...he's handcuffed to a seat.

In just a few chapters, I identified with Alex in more ways than I can count.

The character development that ensues is not the fact that he does the things he does, but how he responds. The mental back-and-forth he has with Jezzie Flanagan is fantastic. The actions he takes in the scenes during the payoff show what a good cop and quick thinker he is.

Does Alex mature over the course of these chapters? No. But Patterson helps me meet Alex where he is.

You too should help your readers meet your character where he or she is. You can't know where your character is until they're on the page.

If you want to review your character's development after you've written the story, that's better. But review the development through DNA by enhancing what's already there—not through a graph, chart, or formula of what someone "thinks" your hero should be.

As I look back on my early novels, the most time I wasted was in plotting character development.

Readers never respond the way you think they will. In fact, they will surprise you.

Don't force your character development. Let it be organic, and remember that the key is in your DNA.

THE MURKY MIDDLE: HOW TO SURVIVE IT

Every writer deals with the "murky middle" in some form. The middle of the book is a large continent, and if you don't have the right tools for the journey, you'll get stuck.

The middle is the #1 place most writers struggle, particularly early on.

You might struggle with the entire middle of the book, or just a few sticky sections where the plotting, pacing, or characters don't feel right. No matter how small, the challenge you face always seems insurmountable at the time.

The murky middle is real, but the reason the middle is murky is misunderstood.

The point of this chapter is to offer you some perspective during those times when nothing in the novel seems to be going your way.

A MINDSET SHIFT THAT MAKES A BIG DIFFERENCE

. . .

Eighty percent of the time, the problem is not your story.

Every novel has a honeymoon phase. No exceptions.

When you start writing your novel, you thrive on extra energy and enthusiasm because you've started something new.

That energy won't last forever. For me personally, I lose my initial momentum after about the 25% mark. No idea why, but it happens every single time.

Here's the perspective I want to share with you because I know it will help you when things get tough: When you are finished with your book, the rough patches won't seem so rough. In fact, they'll look just fine. Once you reach the end of revision, all the issues that seemed like issues magically wash away. Sure, there are still parts that you might wish you could have done better, but when you look back on the book a year or two from now, you're going to feel good about the book, not bad.

What if that's not true? What if the book still looks bad to you?

Then you should let go. You probably suffer from perfectionism.

ELIMINATE PERFECTIONISM FROM YOUR LIFE

I was a perfectionist early in my writing career. I wanted everything to be perfect. Every sentence, every paragraph, every cluster of paragraphs, and every chapter had to be immaculately written and beautiful.

That hurt me because I spent a lot of time on areas that didn't need it. I revised sections that didn't need to be revised, resulting in poorer stories. If I had just listened to my instinct more, I would have written better short stories and books at the very beginning of my career.

You know what ended my perfectionism, though?

I almost died.

When you have a near-death experience, you prioritize things differently. The things that seemed important before I had my experience were irrelevant overnight. A shortlist of those things: what other people think of me, the need to be validated, and the need to write the perfect novel.

Life is short. Crazy short.

After I returned home from the hospital, I tried to write a short story, but I struggled. I remember thinking to myself, "This is bullshit. I could get hit by a bus tomorrow, and what would I have to show for my writing career? A couple of pretty sentences?"

And at that moment, I stopped being a perfectionist. Instead, I focused on creating quality stories, but I learned when to stop. It was hard at first, but for me, it was a life or death situation.

Perfectionism is bad. There are few areas in your writing career where it is a good thing.

You may not have had a near-death experience or a visceral revelation like me, but that's not required.

All you need to know is this: one day, you're going to die. The only things that will matter are the relationships you made with your family and friends, and the legacy you leave behind. Your legacy includes your books, and if you muster up the resolve to finish them, someone could potentially read your book a hundred years from now, and it could completely change their life.

But none of that will happen if you don't take action immediately.

You will be forgotten if you don't take action immediately.

Does that create paranoia for you?

It does for me.

Despite my hard work ethic, resourcefulness, and easygoing personality, one of my character flaws is that I'm paranoid. I worry that time is going to run out for me, that things will be over for me before I can achieve my dreams.

Because of my paranoia, I can never again be a perfectionist.

Now, I'm not telling you that you should be paranoid.

But is there a fire that keeps you going?

So many writers I talk to don't have fire. If you want to be a successful writer, you have to have fire. You've got to be burning inside. When you have fire and purpose, perfectionism goes away.

Because here's another secret: the perfectionism that's important to you isn't important to readers.

Readers don't care about how perfect your outline is, or how pretty your sentences are.

They (mostly) care that your book is well-edited, which is why you hire an editor.

They care about getting value for their money. They work day jobs, have significant others and families, and every book purchase counts.

Most importantly, they care about your characters. And despite what anyone tells you, no character is perfect, both in theory and execution. No reader is perfect, either, so they don't demand absolute perfection in the books they read.

Once, I was speaking at an author conference, and I mentioned to the crowd that I was an introvert, yet I was on stage delivering a presentation anyway. A writer approached me after the presentation and thanked me for sharing that little detail. She shared her story with me about how she overcame her fear of public speaking. She was on stage at her first event, and the moment she opened her mouth, her voice broke and she turned pale. However, she took a moment to focus, and a small piece of advice from a friend got her through the discomfort: in the moment her voice broke, she realized that every single person in the audience wanted her to succeed. They were immediately on her side. She remembered this as she gave her speech. Sure, it was full of ums, ahs, and stuttering. But she conveyed her message, and the audience appreciated what she had to say. Not a single person came up to her and said "you suck." Instead, they congratulated her and engaged her in conversation.

What an incredible metaphor for overcoming perfectionism.

When readers buy your book, they're on your side. They want you to succeed.

So do yourself a favor and lower your standard of excellence if you're a perfectionist. You'll find that interesting things happen when you do.

To bring this back to the murky middle...often, the middle feels bad because you want your book to be perfect. You have this image in your head of what it should look like, but you can't quite get there.

When faced with this problem, most writers will revert to perfectionism, spending more time revising the middle to make it better. Up to a certain point, revision is okay, but you need to know when to stop.

Sometimes, even if the flow of the middle doesn't feel right, there may not be anything wrong with it. It honestly could be just your mind playing tricks on you.

WRITER'S BLOCK: WHAT TO DO ABOUT IT

No writing book would be complete without discussing writer's block.

My book, *Be a Writing Machine*, is all about writer's block, so I know this topic.

Disclaimer: I don't believe in writer's block. Not in the commonly-accepted sense of the term.

I believe that your subconscious (creative voice) knows everything it needs to know about writing a story, and that there are three reasons it gets stuck:

- Lack of inspiration.
- Fear.
- Life events that prevent you from writing because you need to take care of other more urgent matters.

Lack of inspiration usually means that your mind is empty and you need to fill it with content that inspires you.

Fear is deadly because your critical voice will make your creative voice retreat. Fear will also end your writing career if you let it.

Life events are what they are; you can't prevent them, but you can choose how you respond. More often than not, once you attend to the life event standing in your way, the writer's block disappears shortly after. It's your subconscious's way of telling you to press pause.

In this chapter, I will share three tips from *Be a Writing Machine* that are relevant to the murky middle to help you think differently about it.

WRITER'S BLOCK STRATEGY #1: ASK YOURSELF THE TOUGH QUESTIONS, THEN BE QUIET AND LISTEN

. . .

The first murky middle strategy calls for introspection.

Have you ever asked yourself a question?

Have you ever had a conversation with yourself?

So many people I know don't take time for introspection. They claim they "don't have time" for it, or that it seems silly, or that "only weird people do that."

Introspection isn't weird, and it's definitely something you should make time for.

In order to determine where your subconscious is and what kind of help it needs, you need to ask.

Here's how I usually do it. Whenever I am stuck and feel a block coming on, I close my eyes and ask myself one of the following questions:

"What do I need to continue in my story?"

"What's blocking me right now, and what can I do about it?"

"How do I solve this?"

For maximum effect, I ask myself these questions when I am in the shower, driving to work, or falling asleep.

Now, on to answers.

Most people might think that your subconscious will jump up and down and tell you what you need.

"I need you to drink some coffee, please!"

"I need you to have a conversation with the next random stranger you meet!"

"Would you mind taking a nap?"

Unfortunately, it doesn't work that way. Your subconscious doesn't answer questions clearly. The answer will never come to you right away. And it will never come in the format you're expecting.

Also, you have to learn how to silence all the other chattering thoughts in your head. Sometimes they speak so loudly that you can't hear what your subconscious is trying to tell you.

You must learn to identify your subconscious's voice. You'll know it when you hear it. It's not so much a voice as it is a feeling. When you connect with it, you'll feel it guiding you and sometimes controlling your mind as you write.

When the answer comes, you will know. For me, a random thought will usually pop into my head that will solve the issue I'm having. I call it a glimmer—suddenly I "see" a way forward in my story, and my mind expands ever so slightly.

I've learned to be on the lookout for glimmers, and I love that moment when they appear. It gives me a satisfying feeling, like leveling up does in a video game.

Asking the tough questions simply tells your subconscious that you know it needs help. When you do, your subconscious begins a negotiation with the universe to try to figure out how it can proceed.

I heard a saying once that no question ever goes unanswered. Ask a question to the universe, and it will answer you in its own way.

You just have to be quiet and listen.

WRITER'S BLOCK STRATEGY #2: MEDITATION

Enough has been written about the medical and spiritual benefits of meditation that I won't summarize them here.

But I will talk about how you can use meditation as a writer.

Meditation is the perfect way to ask yourself questions. It's also the perfect way for you to learn how to listen to yourself.

Meditation is easy too. Find a quiet room, a comfortable chair, set a timer, sit down, and close your eyes.

Once, at a teenage boy's camp, my counselor facilitated a devilish exercise to show us just how disconnected we were from nature.

He told us to close our eyes and be silent for one minute.

At the end of the minute, we were told to raise our hand.

I'll never forget what happened next. I closed my eyes and became aware of the train wreck going on inside my head. I could not shut my mind off. The inside of my head was filled with sights, sounds, and smells. I was itchy and I fought the urge to scratch my face. I remembered things that I forgot to pack. I tried to count to 60, but I lost focus somewhere around 15.

I ended up raising my hand, not knowing how much time had passed.

I opened my eyes, and other boys were grinning at me with their hands up. Others still had their eyes closed, mental anguish clearly visible on their faces.

My counselor stood there with a stopwatch and a smirk on his face, waiting for everyone to raise their hands.

About two minutes later, everyone finished.

He then told us that the first person raised their hand after 30 seconds, and the last person raised their hand at three minutes.

I raised mine somewhere around 30 seconds...

That was eye-opening for me.

You see, we don't always have a true concept of time. With technology and our fast-paced lives, we live quickly, which disconnects us with time and, most importantly, our inner selves.

Meditation helps you reconnect with yourself. It's one of the few things that you can do every day and see incredible mental, spiritual, and health improvements quickly.

I'm not advocating that you meditate for hours at a time.

I meditate for five minutes every morning, just before I write.

I sit in my recliner in my office, set a timer on my phone, and close my eyes.

I ask myself, "Where was I in my work-in-progress?" (Or, I ask myself one of the tough questions in the last strategy.)

The most recent scene in my story flashes in my mind's eye.

Then I sit still and listen to my subconscious answer. Sometimes it will show me what's next. Other times it will be silent and I can focus on clearing my mind of any clutter.

In any case, the goal is to go with the flow.

When my timer goes off, I'm at complete peace. I can usually start writing quickly after my meditation sessions.

Daily meditation is good for your mind. It's lubricant that keeps your subconscious operating without friction. It will help you get through your murky middle too.

WRITER'S BLOCK STRATEGY #3: MICROFOCUS

When the words won't flow, it can be agonizing. You don't know what to do, and you don't have the inspiration.

When the other strategies aren't working, and you're losing hope, try this one.

It's called micro focusing.

You visualize the spot in the story where you are stuck, and you focus on the next sentence.

Literally. The next sentence.

Don't focus on the story. Don't focus on the character. Just focus on the next sentence.

Write it and don't think about it.

Then write the next sentence.

I make this sound easy, but trust me, when you're in the moment, it's really hard. In fact, it's so hard that you'll often wonder how you'll ever finish the novel. Trust me, I get it.

When you're not inspired, sometimes you have to sit in the

chair and get work done. It's hard, but there's no way around it unfortunately.

The key here is to put your butt in the chair and don't let yourself get up until you write a substantial amount. That's the hard part.

This is also a strategy you can use to combat fear.

THE LAST MINDSET SHIFT YOU NEED TO KNOW

You're probably wondering why all of the strategies I gave in this chapter are mindset-based and not technical.

Aside from the advice I will give you in the next section, the murky middle usually has nothing to do with writing craft.

Eighty percent of the time, it has nothing to do with your story.

It has everything to do with your belief system about yourself, your writing, and how well you can cope with difficulty.

Follow the mindset strategies I talked about to change your perspective.

But the last mindset shift you need to know is called reframing.

When you reframe, you take a bad situation and turn it into a positive one.

Using this technique, I've learned to be endlessly positive when it comes to my writing.

Here are some examples of how you can reframe pitfalls during your murky middle.

. . .

SITUATION: One of my chapters in the middle is significantly shorter than the rest.

INITIAL THOUGHT: Readers are going to notice. I need to add some meat to the ending!

REFRAMED PERSPECTIVE: A shorter chapter could be interesting to readers; maybe it will keep them turning the page.

SITUATION: My sidekick's subplot doesn't have the emotional intensity I think it needs, even after revision.

INITIAL THOUGHT: I need to add more scenes.

REFRAMED PERSPECTIVE: Maybe it doesn't quite pack the punch I wanted, but maybe it does. I've done everything I can do in writing the DNA. I'll let the readers decide.

SITUATION: This sucks. I can't do this.

INITIAL THOUGHT: I'm an imposter. I'm faking it as a writer.

REFRAMED PERSPECTIVE: Most people never make it as far as I have. When I'm done, I'll be even further along than most. Just gotta keep going.

SITUATION: Writer's block...again.

INITIAL THOUGHT: The universe doesn't want me to write this damn novel.

REFRAMED PERSPECTIVE: What can I learn from this bout of writer's block? How will this ultimately make my story better?

SITUATION: I don't know what to write next.

INITIAL THOUGHT: I don't know what to do because this is really scary.

REFRAMED PERSPECTIVE: I bet there are times when my favorite authors don't know what to write next. If they can deal with it, so can I.

SITUATION: I worry that my science is wrong.

INITIAL THOUGHT: I better research space travel more.

REFRAMED PERSPECTIVE: Ray Bradbury got his science TERRIBLY wrong in The Martian Chronicles, and he's considered to be one of the greatest science fiction writers of all time. If he can get a few things wrong, so can I.

Reframing is important. If you have a personality type that tends to go negative, this will be harder for you, maybe impossible.

But the writing life is full of setbacks and barriers. If you can't learn to reframe your problems so that you can find a solution, then I'm sorry, but you won't last. If you do last, you'll risk a life of bitterness, because trust me, there are going to be more setbacks than you can imagine.

Being negative and bitter is no way to live, especially because writing is an escape. Books should bring happiness to readers. You can't deliver happiness to readers if you aren't happy yourself.

Keep your writing fun. Reframe every problem you face into an opportunity, even if it feels unnatural.

Do this, and you'll find your way through every murky middle, every single time.

The hard part is changing your mindset.

. . .

CRAFT TIPS FOR THE MURKY MIDDLE

There will be times when there is an actual problem with your murky middle, and you need to apply craft techniques to solve it.

In my opinion, it's best if you focus on the writing and power through the pain.

The techniques that come next are left-brained and can impair your creative voice if you're not careful. But I share them because there may be a time when you need to use them.

The best advice I can give you is to resist the temptation to rush through the middle and fix it later in revision. If you do that, you'll spend twice as much time editing.

However murky your middle looks during the writing process, it will be twice as bad in revision if you don't address the root of the problem in real-time. This is because when you're writing, you're in the right mindset. Your creative voice is roaming and playing, and it's better equipped to help you through the problem. If you wait until revision, your creative voice will be off playing in other places, and it will be very hard to get back into the same creative state you were in when you were writing your middle.

Let's go over some unorthodox but effective craft strategies for navigating the murky middle if you get stuck.

SUBPLOTS

. . .

Subplots are important. They reveal a lot about the hero and supporting characters. But you can run into several issues:

- The subplot runs too long.
- The subplot runs too short.
- The subplot feels tangential.
- The subplot feels like its own story.

The first thing I would gauge is whether the subplot "feels" right. Does the content on the page make sense in context with the story? Does it pay off either later in the book or in the series? Listen to your instinct and obey it. I would make sure you understand that before you make any changes. When you take a hard look at the story, you may not actually have a problem.

That's worth repeating again: you may not actually have a problem.

If the subplot "feels" too long or too short, do some simple math. How many words is it compared to the rest of your novel? There's no rule for this, but it will give you some perspective.

If you have a subplot that collectively is 10,000 words and your novel is 60,000 words, that might be just right. If your subplot is 30,000 words and your novel is 90,000 words, that might not be, since a third of your novel would be subplot that doesn't contribute to the overall story.

Use the math to give yourself some perspective. Again, I wouldn't apply any rules here. Some people are going to read that last paragraph and then think their subplot has to be within a certain ratio. That's not what I'm saying.

But I would be looking for extremely high and low percentages as red flags. For example, if 40-50% of your book is subplot, then you're probably doing something wrong. Maybe that subplot should be its own novel, novella, or short story. If 5% of your book is subplot, should it even be there?

But as I said, you may not need to do any cutting.

Apply this test to determine whether you should address the issue with your subplot:

- If you took the subplot away, could the novel stand on its own?
- If the answer yes, then you have a non-critical subplot. Is there a pay off that makes the subplot worth it? (For example, does it develop a supporting character to help them get ready for the final battle?) Just simply "revealing" details about a character is not enough. There has to be a real purpose to the subplot, and there has to be character development.
- If yes, then you have a critical subplot. I would advise you not to cut it. Instead, consider your DNA and whether certain sections may be contributing to the problem. Look at each instance of the subplot in isolation—are there certain parts within those that are unnecessary? For example, do you start a chapter too early? Little strategic clippings or additions here and there might be just what you need.

Here's an example I encountered with subplots, and why I learned to trust my instinct.

In my Android X series, my android hero, X, has a human engineer sidekick named Shortcut. X is stoic (as you'd expect an android to be), but Shortcut is vibrant and full of energy. He's a young engineer fresh out of college, and he believes that he should be an engineering manager. Before the story begins, he applies for a manager and gets rejected for it, which makes him act childish and embarrass himself in front of Commander Fahrens, the leader of the android sector.

The subplot in the story is Shortcut trying to power himself up so he can prove himself to the commander. He desires to be better, faster, and smarter—and he'll do anything for it. He visits a clandestine "doctor" who installs nanotechnology "enhancements" in his brain—a common thing in the year 2300. The only problem is that Shortcut is addicted to nano enhancements. He has dozens and dozens of them, more than is medically safe. The subplot is him secretly medicating himself and hiding his declining health from X.

Guess what?

I almost cut this subplot. I worried that it didn't add value to the story.

My instinct told me otherwise. Thank God I listened!

To this very day, readers absolutely love Shortcut because of his subplot. In fact, they love Shortcut so much that they've asked me to write a series from his perspective.

Remember, listen to your instinct!

ANOTHER IDEA: WRITE OUT OF ORDER

This is likely a foreign concept to most writers, but it is an incredible way to break out of the murky middle.

Writing out of sequence is a little strange, but I've done it effectively many times.

The great thing about writing out of order is that it can unlock some passion and creativity. Maybe the section you're working on is boring you for some reason. Maybe you can write like crazy if you jump three chapters ahead.

Quick caveat: this DOES NOT mean to rush or write sloppily. Don't do that!

But if you skip ahead and see some success, you can use that momentum to sail back and write your way through the rough patches.

If you're an outliner, congratulations! You can do this without any trouble. After all, you already know what you're going to write (that in and of itself could be the very reason you're stuck or bored, but I won't go there).

If you're a pantser, you're probably sweating right now. Is it harder for you? Yes, but not insurmountable. Every time I've written out of sequence was when I was pantsing, so it can be done.

Believe it or not, I wrote my entire Galaxy Mavericks space opera series out of order. I wrote Book 2 first, then 1, 4, 3, 5, 6, 7, 8, and 9. Crazy, but fun!

IF IN DOUBT, ADD MORE VILLAIN TIME

There's a saying by the famous crime writer Raymond Chandler: "If your plot is flagging, have a man come in with a gun."

I love that quote. This technique works like magic too.

You don't have to insert a man with a gun into your story, but you can give the villain more chapter time.

Maybe you have the villain show up and cause even more trouble than you originally planned for. That builds tension, which is sometimes what a murky middle needs. Or maybe the villain sends one of his or her minions to thwart the hero. What that looks like for you depends on your novel. But if you can find a way to do it that doesn't feel forced, you can almost never go wrong with introducing more tension into your story.

It really is that simple.

ONE LAST THING

Don't stress out over murky middles. When you're in the moment, you're going to feel pretty terrible. You're going to feel like you can't do it and that you're a fraud. You'll wonder how you'll ever get the energy to continue writing your book. You might even feel a little angry and frustrated that the story didn't come to you more easily. Even worse, you might feel guilty for spending time away from your friends, family, and children, only to be working on a failing novel.

Those feelings are normal. In fact, until you've written a lot of novels, they are a disproportionate part of the process because you have to learn how to control them.

Whenever you feel down or unhappy, stop what you're doing, reframe, and return. If that means taking a walk, take a walk. If that means taking a nap, take a nap. If it's eleven o'clock at night and you're stumped, go to bed.

Just don't procrastinate. Always, always, always make yourself engage with your story, even if it doesn't want to engage with you.

Those feelings will pass. They always do. But when you're in the moment, you can't see past them.

Trust me: I've done this over forty times, so I know what I'm talking about!

You're almost there, and you're already a champion in my eyes.

You've learned how to open your book, write good chapter openings and endings, the basic principles of DNA, the ins and outs of character development, and most important of all, how to wade through the murky middle and come out on the other side.

What's on the other side?

The final battle, of course.

That's right, it's time to prepare for the epic showdown between your hero and villain.

A SIMPLE BUT EFFECTIVE FINAL BATTLE CHECKLIST

I love final battles. Few sections in a novel allow you to be truly artistic than the epic battle with the villain.

Growing up, I played Japanese RPGs, and the final battles

were some of the most epic and artistic I've ever seen, so much that I adopted the general principles behind them in my own work. Readers have given me feedback that my battles are unique and interesting, so hopefully, I'm doing a few things right!

You ultimately have to define this checklist and make it appropriate for your book and genre, but here are the elements I believe every good final battle should have:

- High stakes. Don't be humble. If you're writing science fiction & fantasy, the fate of the world is usually at stake, so don't be afraid to dream up something crazy. If you're writing romance, it's the final test of love, so make it unique. If you're writing mystery or thrillers, someone's life is almost always at stake.
- A unique setting. Bonus points if the setting has critical importance to the story.
- Teamwork. The hero and supporting characters are working together, and their lives are being challenged.

I won't give any spoilers or tell you which of my books these are in, but here are a couple of final battles I've done:

- Showdown in an underwater skyscraper in the middle of the Arctic Ocean, with the final battle taking place in a lab with a view of a dead, sunken city in the frigid ocean.
- A nightmare inside an innocent person's mind created by the villain that gets progressively worse and deadly for the heroine. Only one can survive, but both the heroine and villain can die.

- Legal battle in a courtroom between heaven and hell, with a judge and jury of devils and angels.

My personal writing philosophy is to dazzle the reader with ridiculously high stakes (almost to the point of absurdity), a unique setting with sensory details that border on the verge of sensory overload, intense emotions, and screen time for all the major characters. I never go overboard; I always stop right at the line.

Okay, I lied—there was one time I went waaaaay overboard with a final battle, but the risk paid off...

As you think about your final battle, you don't have to follow my philosophy, but I do want you to think big.

In many respects, this is going to be the one scene your readers remember. Make it memorable.

ENDING: CLIFFHANGER OR NOT?

A QUICK WORD ON ENDINGS.

How you end your story is up to you. I can't give you a checklist or a how-to on it. But you do have a couple of very important decisions to make:

- Is the novel standalone or a series?
- Should you end on a cliffhanger?

STANDALONE VS. SERIES

You should know if your novel is a standalone or a series. You may not know when you start it, but by the time you've reached the ending, you should have a sense of whether you're done artistically or if you want to keep going.

The pros of standalone novels are that they're a self-contained experience. I liken it to eating a full-course meal.

When you're done, you either feel satisfied or like you over ate, but the point is that you're finished.

The cons of standalone novels are that unless you're writing literary fiction, they're somewhat out of vogue in this new world of publishing. A notable exception among genre fiction is novellas.

Think about your standalone like this:

- Is it a closed standalone, meaning there will not be any further continuation of the main character?
- Is it an open standalone, meaning that you're giving yourself the option of continuing the series in the future if you want to? A lot of writers overlook this, but it's particularly smart if you're not sure if you want to continue with a series. You end the novel, the reader feels satisfied, but you leave the door half-open for future adventures.

There's no right or wrong answer here. Some genres lend themselves better to standalone, like mystery, thriller and romance. Sometimes, a standalone may be your only option.

For series, it's a little more straightforward. You simply have to choose where you want to end the story and how. Series are king right now, and it's impossible to deny that they make more money.

But you can have series where the books are standalones (like the Jack Reacher series), and you can have series where the books are continuous and need to be read in order (like the Harry Potter series).

My general rule of thumb is not to mix types within a single world. If you have a mystery series and you're going to do standalones, do standalones for that series and character. If you have a space opera and you're going to do series, do series for that

space opera. You don't want to confuse your readers from book
to book.

CLIFFHANGERS: SHOULD YOU?

Up to this point, we've talked about cliffhangers at the chapter
level, which in my opinion are non-negotiable for most genres.

Consider the numerous benefits of a cliffhanger ending for
your book:

- It builds suspense for the next novel.
- It entices readers to buy your next novel, usually in
  an impulsive, can't-help-myself kind of way.
- It increases the chances of readers staying up past
  their bedtime to keep reading your next book.
- It increases the potential that your novel will have
  word-of-mouth appeal. ("Did you finish the ending
  of that novel? Duuuude!")

Yet, some readers hate cliffhangers at the book level. In fact,
there are groups of readers who won't even buy a book if they
know it ends with a cliffhanger. I believe they're a minority, but
they're real.

The reasons they hate cliffhangers are legit. It's usually
because an author somewhere screwed up or got greedy.

Here's why some readers hate cliffhangers:

- A writer ended the story on a cliffhanger and died
  before finishing the series, or decided they didn't
  want to write it anymore, leaving the reader to
  wonder what if. Readers hate that. I, too, have been

burned, and I usually won't buy a book until the series is complete. Hence, why I release my entire series at the same time.

- A writer ended a novel too soon and made readers have to buy the next book in order to find out what happens, making them feel like they were duped.
- A writer ended the story on a cliffhanger, only for that "cliffhanger" not to be a real cliffhanger. It's the equivalent of saying "Just kidding. Thanks for the money, though. Keep reading, and enjoy!"

The lesson here: don't be a knucklehead. Write and give your story in good faith. If you write a cliffhanger, tie up major loose ends prior to the cliffhanger, and focus on making the cliffhanger the natural result of the hero and villain playing a game of tug-of-war.

Another lesson: if you're going to write a cliffhanger, don't leave readers hanging. Write your next book quickly. You don't want them cursing your name if you were to get hit by a bus tomorrow.

If you treat your readers with respect and end your stories tastefully, there is no reason why you shouldn't do a cliffhanger. They work, and they make money.

WHAT ABOUT THE OTHER STUFF?

Pacing.

Point of View.

Character voice.

Suspense.

Minor characters.

Villains.

Those, and all the other elements of the writing craft. What about them?

For your first novel or few, I don't know that you need to worry about them.

You likely have a lot of problems right now, and these elements are probably the least of them.

If you want to play the game, you need to master the basics. And honestly, it can take the rest of your writing career to get the basics right. I know I'm still working on them.

I threw a lot at you in this chapter, enough to last you a long time. I'll perhaps do books on the other elements, but my belief is that if you can learn to master the art of DNA, openings, endings, character development, and the overall process of starting and finishing a novel, you'll write some kickass stories.

Another truth is that if you learn to start looking for new elements in the books you read, you'll be able to pick them up pretty quick using the framework I taught you in this book.

The important keys:

- Learn how to look for new elements (i.e. pacing, point of View, etc.).
- Learn how to pick them apart and put them back together again.
- Learn how to look for and come up with variations on what you see.

If you learn to do those things, you can teach yourself how to learn virtually any writing craft element quickly.

The hard part is mastery.

You've finished your novel. Congratulations!

What now?

I suspect that most of you reading this plan to revise your novel.

Revision is fine, but I have some contrarian views on it.

First, I believe in a free market style of revision. This means reading regularly, a purposeful and directed study of the craft when you're not writing, writing your story correctly the first time, listening to your instinct, and finally, only revising parts of the novel that truly need to be touched.

I do not believe that there is any objective way for you to know if a rewrite or edit will be effective. I don't believe in developmental editing because I have not seen any conclusive evidence that it helps you write an (objectively) better story.

I believe in studying the craft like a professional and letting your instincts guide you.

I believe that if you study the craft and let your instincts guide you, you will write good stories and get better with each book.

I believe that readers vote with their wallets. They buy

novels that were extensively rewritten just as frequently as they buy novels that were written in one draft, and there's no secret or shortcut that will help you predict whether they'll buy your book.

I believe in letting them decide whether your novel is good, hence why I call it free market revision.

This means that the following revision types are off-limits for me personally:

* Developmental editing (with one caveat; keep reading)
* Major rewrites
* More than two rounds of revision

My caveat with developmental editing is that I don't believe in paying thousands of dollars for something that you can't objectively prove is effective. However, I believe paying a beta reader (someone who actually reads books in your genre) is a fantastic revision tool.

And yes, I said paying a beta reader. Paying them a small fee increases the chances that they'll follow through with their promise to read your book. I've been burned by beta readers more times than I can count.

I don't like rewriting. Period. Nothing makes me want to throw my computer across the room than scrapping what I wrote and starting again. It's much better to just slow down and get it right the first time (within reason; don't be a perfectionist).

The only time I begrudgingly accept rewrites is if I write something later in the story that changes something I wrote earlier in the novel. When that happens, I stop immediately and do the rewrite. I almost never do rewriting in revision, unless I completely missed a plot hole, which has only happened once.

I also don't like too many rounds of revision because of the law of diminishing returns. At one point, you just have to separate yourself from the novel and call it done. There's a difference between wanting to write a clean manuscript for your editor and endlessly tinkering with stuff that doesn't matter. You can only revise so much before it stops being effective.

A lot of writers believe that the magic happens in revision. I disagree. For me, the magic happens when I'm writing, and I wouldn't have it any other way.

Entire books have been written on revision, and while some of them are valid, I believe that the writing community places too much emphasis on revision. We make it into this daunting task that requires dozens of drafts and meticulous perfectionism when it's really just a simple validation of what you've written.

Remember: you're a writer, not an editor. You can't do both jobs. That's why you hire good editors to help you with your story, mechanics, and proofreading.

Don't overthink it.

In fact, I challenge you to think more simply about revision. I'm not telling you that you shouldn't revise, but I am asking you consider if the time spent on sixteen drafts is worth it, or if you could just as easily accomplish the same result in five, or maybe less.

I know that most of you reading this won't agree with me 100%, so I've found a common ground. Here are my recommendations for revision that will help you revise your story in the best possible productive way without getting mired in details.

A SIMPLE REVISION WORKFLOW

1. Hire a paid beta reader to give you feedback and

incorporate the advice that makes the most sense for your story.

1. Allow yourself three (3) rounds of revision. One for dialogue, one for narrative, and one for action & story flow.
2. Limit each of those rounds to a hard time limit. What you choose is up to you, but don't let this take weeks or months. If you followed my advice and wrote cleanly and correctly (no sloppy first drafts), then this should be a short process. Move briskly through each pass and obey your time limit.
3. Spell-check the novel in Microsoft Word (or whatever spell-checker you have).
4. Consider using a tool like ProWritingAid or Grammarly to catch additional spelling errors. This is optional.
5. Hire a copyeditor and incorporate their edits.
6. Hire a proofreader and incorporate their edits.
7. Spell-check the novel one last time, either with Word or ProWritingAid or Grammarly. Using both is overkill in my opinion, but you can do that if you want since it won't take you too much additional time.
8. Publish.

Despite my contrarian views, I do not skimp on quality or professionalism. This method gets fresh eyes on your work and shows your commitment to your readers by ensuring the highest possible quality with fewest typos.

I just believe in producing novels quickly and well.

This workflow can help you do the same.

THANKS so much for reading this book. I hope it helps you write world class stories cleaner, better, and faster.

To review, I want you to develop a commitment to mastering the following:

- Chapter openings
- Chapter endings
- Dialogue, narrative, and action (DNA)
- Sensory details
- Character development
- Writing good middles right the first time
- Awesome and epic final battles
- Satisfying endings

Pay attention to each of these when you read your next book for pleasure.

When I learned these things and started looking for them in my daily reading, it completely elevated my consciousness. It was as if someone took the blinders off my eyes. Now I can't unsee them any time I read a book, and I know how to spot and analyze the techniques that successful writers use in their novels, which ultimately makes my novels better. I want that for you too.

For next steps, I want you to do two things.

First, check out the Resources section in the next chapter. I have created YouTube videos on almost every topic in this book, and I explore them in other ways that you might find helpful. I've also compiled helpful books, podcasts, and links to help you on your writing journey.

Second, subscribe to my YouTube channel, Author Level Up. If you liked this book, you'll love my videos because the advice I give in this book is exactly the kind of videos I publish every week. In fact, I put together a playlist of videos that relate to this book.

Writing a novel shouldn't be scary. It should be an exploratory process where you learn about yourself and create a story that makes a difference in your readers' lives. You may not know what your journey entails, but you can and should embrace it, and have fun.

So embrace this wild journey you're on. And have fun.

I've taught you everything I know.

Now go write.

Peace, love, and light,
M.L. Ronn

RESOURCES MENTIONED IN THIS BOOK

Here is a list of resources mentioned in this book to help you on your writing journey.

IMPORTANT LINKS

My YouTube Channel: www.authorlevelup.com

WRITING APPS

Microsoft Office

Ulysses: www.ulysses.app

Scrivener: www.authorlevelup.com/scrivener

. . .

Evernote: www.evernote.com

WRITING BOOKS

Outlining Your Novel

The Hero With a Thousand Faces by Joseph Campbell

Screenplay by Syd Field

Story Engineering by Larry Brooks

Write Your Novel from the Middle by James Scott Bell

How to Write a Novel Using the Snowflake Method by Randy Ingermanson

Lester   Dent's   Plot   Formula: www.
authorlevelup.com/lesterdent

Techniques of the Selling Writer by Dwight V. Swain

. . .

Write. Publish. Repeat by Sean Platt, Johnny B. Truant and Dave Wright

I've gathered all of the books into a shopping list that you can use to check them out: www.authorlevelup.com/firstnovelbooks

WRITING CRAFT COURSES

I highly recommend these courses to help you improve your craft. I have taken them personally.

WMG Workshops by Dean Wesley Smith and Kristine Kathryn Rusch: www.authorlevelup.com/wmg

VIDEOS:

I have over 200 videos on my YouTube channel, Author Level Up, that address many of the topics I talk about in this book.

You can find all of the videos below in this section gathered in a single playlist here: www. authorlevelup.com/firstnovelvideos

Basically, the playlist is like a free course that goes more in-depth into the material I talk about in this book.

. . .

FREQUENTLY ASKED QUESTION VIDEOS:

Advanced Time Management

Creating Author Systems Part 1

Creating Author Systems Part 2

Writing with a Full-Time Job

How I Fit Everything In

How to Come Up With Story Ideas

Should I Quit Writing My Novel?

WRITING TOOLS VIDEOS

Top 5 FREE Writing Apps for Mac

Best PAID Writing Apps for Mac

. . .

Buying a Writing App: Shopping List

Scrivener Essentials (Video Playlist)

Ulysses Essentials (Video Playlist)

Scrivener vs. Ulysses Cage Match

Grammarly Review

ProWritingAid Review

Grammarly vs ProWriting Aid App Battle

PLANNING YOUR NOVEL VIDEOS

10 Ways to Outline Your Novel

How to Outline a Novel in Scrivener

Writing into the Dark: Write a Novel Without an Outline

. . .

Writing Without an Outline

WRITING YOUR NOVEL VIDEOS

How to Write a Novel Step-by-Step

How to Learn Fiction Writing: 10 Things They Don't Teach in School

What to Do When You Can't Write

Can't Finish Your Novel? Try This

Working Through Fear

REVISING YOUR NOVEL VIDEOS

Self-Editing Your Book

Developmental Editing: Worth It?

How to Edit a Novel in Scrivener

• • •

MY BOOKS USED FOR EXAMPLES

Death Marked, Book 1 in the Modern Necromancy series: www.michaellaronn.com/deathmarked

Honor's Reserve, Book 1 in the Galaxy Mavericks series: www. michaellaronn.com/honorsreserve

HERE's an excerpt from the next book in this series, *Be a Writing Machine: Write Faster and Smarter, Beat Writer's Block, and Be Prolific.*

Let's skip the fluffy stuff for a minute and talk about the two simple things you're going to learn in this book.

First, you're going to learn how to write books faster. Way faster. This will be easy.

Second, you're going to learn how to write smarter. This will be hard. Crazy hard. But you will be better for it.

When you're done with this book, you'll have a step-by-step roadmap on how to become the prolific writer you've always wanted to be.

You'll be a writing machine.

What if you could develop a consistent daily writing habit and finish a new novel every few weeks? Every few *days*? What would that mean for your writing career?

We all know that writing more books means more readers and therefore more money. But for many of us, just writing the next chapter is a struggle.

Writing isn't easy. If it was, then everyone would be prolific.

There are tricks to make the words flow easier. Fortunately, it doesn't involve any extra intelligence or wisdom.

I have used the strategies in this book to write 6-8 books on average every year since 2014. I have written dozens of novels in the same amount of time it takes many authors to write a few. My novels range from 40,000 to 70,000 words. The techniques in this book will help you with any fiction genre.

You're going to learn a simple system that you can adapt to suit your own lifestyle and career goals. It doesn't matter whether you're a part-time or a full-time author. All you need is an open mind and a willingness to try something new.

A Little about Me

· · ·

Here's my story and why I'm qualified to write this book.

In July 2012, my wife rushed me to the emergency room. I was experiencing horrible stomach cramps, so bad I couldn't even see straight. Little did I know that the restaurant I'd visited the night before had served me tainted food, resulting in the worst food poisoning of my life.

I'll spare you the details of my hospital visit, but while I was there, I caught an infection.

I spent an entire month doped up on morphine, staring at a wall. I had a lot of time to think about my life.

Until then, I had been a sometime writer. I wrote whenever the muse moved me. I wasn't serious about it.

Something on that hospital bed made me change my mind.

I had a spiritual awakening. Among my many hallucinations, I visualized myself as a published author. It made me so happy—I felt an incredible euphoria just thinking about it. (Okay, the euphoria probably came from the morphine, but hey, details...)

I swore right then and there on that hospital bed that I would become a serious writer, no matter what.

Fortunately, I beat the infection and escaped from the hospital. The very week I came home, an article came out on the front page of *USA Today* about the particular strain of bacteria that I had, and how it was killing an alarming amount of people all over the United States.

Basically, I could have died.

That was life-changing for me.

The next week, I remember sitting down at my kitchen table and trying to write a short story. I didn't know how to start it, and I stared at a blank screen for hours.

I remember an intense wave of fear. My inner critic kicked in.

"You'll never be able to write," it said. "This story will fail. Give up now before you embarrass yourself."

I remember thinking, "Why am I scared? I just spent a month in the hospital on my deathbed and wasn't scared of dying, so why the hell am I scared about writing this short story?"

Something clicked.

Then I stopped being afraid of just about everything in my life.

Compared to what I had been through, "fear," in the writer's sense of the word, stopped scaring me. I learned how to fight my fear every time it tried to stop me.

And then, one morning, four years later, I woke up and realized I had written over 40 books, with no signs of slowing down.

I wrote those books while becoming a father for the first time.

I wrote those books while climbing the corporate ladder at a Fortune 100 insurance company in the United States, with management-level responsibility.

I wrote those books while attending law school in the evenings.

I wrote those books while being a friend, father, son, husband, and all the thousand other things my loved ones needed me to be.

I wrote those books while hosting a podcast, running a YouTube channel, mentoring other authors, and finding ways to give back to the indie author community as a liaison for the Alliance of Independent Authors.

If anyone should have a thousand excuses not to write, it should be me. If you look at my life, it's a miracle that I can even *think* about writing.

But that's enough about my credentials. I just wanted to get those out of the way to show you that I know the topic of writing fast and smart. And I know it well.

If I can do this, it's only right for me to share some of my secrets so that you can do it too.

Quick Overview of This Book's Structure

- The **Mindset** chapter will teach you how you need to adapt your mindset in order to reach new levels of productivity. I can't promise I won't go hippie on you, but I can promise that you'll get a fresh perspective that you haven't seen before.
- The **Tools** chapter will show you what tools I use to hit crazy word counts every day.
- The **Time Management** chapter will teach you how to organize your limited time and make the most of it.
- The **Write Smart** chapter teaches you how to be smart about your novel writing. It will give you a prolific author's perspective on what you can do to produce high numbers of books year after year.
- The **Writer's Block** chapter is the most important in the book. I will show you the root causes of writer's block and my strategies on beating it every time. The latter part of this section is organized into quick hit strategies that you can refer to whenever you find yourself in a rough patch in your work in progress.

My goal for you is to pull back the curtain on how I do it and give you a different perspective on writing fast.

Remember, prolific isn't just about writing one book fast. It's about producing book after book after book, rain or shine, no matter what. It's about learning how to be systematic.

Proficient fiction writers will benefit the most from this book. If you've been through the novel writing process a few times, then the strategies in this book will make more sense to you. If you don't write fiction, you can still use the strategies here, but know that your mileage may vary.

If you're in this for the long haul and are ready to take your word counts to new, consistent heights, then read on.

Want to read more?

Grab your copy of *Be a Writing Machine* today. Available in ebook, paperback, and audiobook formats at your favorite retailer: www.authorlevelup.com/beawritingmachine

Science fiction and fantasy on the wild side!

M.L. Ronn (Michael La Ronn) is the author of many science fiction and fantasy novels including *The Good Necromancer*, *Android X*, and *The Last Dragon Lord* series.

In 2012, a life-threatening illness made him realize that storytelling was his #1 passion. He's devoted his life to writing ever since, making up whatever story makes him fall out of his chair laughing the hardest. Every day.

Learn more about Michael
www.authorlevelup.com (for writers)
www.michaellaronn.com (fiction)

Books for Writers

Indie Author Confidential (Series)
    How to Write Your First Novel
    Be a Writing Machine
    Mental Models for Writers
    The Indie Writer's Encyclopedia
    The Indie Author Atlas
    The Indie Author Bestiary
    The Reader's Bill of Rights
    The Self-Publishing Compendium
    150 Self-Publishing Questions Answered
    Authors, Steal This Book
    The Indie Author Strategy Guide
    How to Dictate a Book
    Advanced Author Editing
    Keep Your Books Selling
    The Author Estate Handbook
    The Author Heir Handbook

Interactive Fiction: How to Engage Readers and Push the Boundaries of Story Telling
Indie Poet Rock Star
Indie Poet Formatting
2016 Indie Author State of the Union

More Books for Writers:

www.authorlevelup.com/books

Fiction:

www.michaellaronn.com/books